Paper P6
**Advanced Taxation
(Finance Act 2015)**

For September 2016 to March 2017
Examination Sittings

Pocket Notes

British library cataloguing-in-publication data

A catalogue record for this book is available from the British Library.

Published by:
Kaplan Publishing UK
Unit 2 The Business Centre
Molly Millars Lane
Wokingham
Berkshire
RG41 2QZ

ISBN 978-1-78415-251-2

© Kaplan Financial Limited, 2016

Printed and bound in Great Britain.

The text in this material and any others made available by any Kaplan Group company does not amount to advice on a particular matter and should not be taken as such. No reliance should be placed on the content as the basis for any investment or other decision or in connection with any advice given to third parties. Please consult your appropriate professional adviser as necessary. Kaplan Publishing Limited and all other Kaplan group companies expressly disclaim all liability to any person in respect of any losses or other claims, whether direct, indirect, incidental, consequential or otherwise arising in relation to the use of such materials.

All rights reserved. No part of this publication may be reproduced, stored in a retrieval system, or transmitted, in any form or by any means, electronic, mechanical, photocopying, recording or otherwise, without the prior written permission of Kaplan Publishing.

Contents

paper P6

		Reference to Complete text chapter	Page Number
Chapter 1	Income tax – overview and investment income	1, 3	1
Chapter 2	Employment income – income tax and national insurance	2	15
Chapter 3	Relief for pensions	4	37
Chapter 4	Capital gains tax – introduction	6, 7	43
Chapter 5	Capital gains tax – shares and securities	8	57
Chapter 6	Capital gains tax – reliefs	9	67
Chapter 7	Stamp taxes	6, 8	91
Chapter 8	Inheritance tax	11-13	95
Chapter 9	Personal tax – overseas aspects	10, 13	123
Chapter 10	Trusts	14	149
Chapter 11	Ethics, personal financial management and self-assessment	3, 15, 16	159
Chapter 12	Personal tax planning	2, 5, 13	187
Chapter 13	Business tax	17-19	201
Chapter 14	Value added tax	20, 21	235

Advanced taxation

		Reference to Complete text chapter	Page Number
Chapter 15	Corporation tax – liability and losses	22-24	26
Chapter 16	Groups – corporation tax and VAT	27, 29	28
Chapter 17	Overseas issues – corporation tax and VAT	21, 28	30
Chapter 18	Business finance and tax planning for companies	25, 26, 29	32
Index			I

Preface

These Pocket Notes contain the key points you need to know for the exam, presented in a unique way that makes revision easy and effective.

Written by experienced lecturers and authors, these Pocket Notes break down content into manageable chunks to maximise your concentration.

Quality and accuracy are of the utmost importance to us so if you spot an error in any of our products, please send an email to mykaplanreporting@kaplan.com with full details, or follow the link to the feedback form in MyKaplan.

Our Quality Co-ordinator will work with our technical team to verify the error and take action to ensure it is corrected in future editions.

The exam

Section A (60%)

- 2 compulsory questions:

    Question 1: 35 Marks, including 4 professional marks

    Question 2: 25 Marks

Section B (40%)

- A choice of two questions out of three, with each question attracting 20 marks.

The entire syllabus can be tested in either section A or section B.

Questions will be scenario based and will normally involve consideration of more than one tax, together with some elements of planning and the interaction of taxes.

Computations will normally only be required in support of explanations or advice and not in isolation.

The examination time is 3 hours and 15 minutes.

Topics which are not tested at F6 and are new to P6 will be frequently examined. However, candidates will also need a thorough knowledge and understanding of the basic tax rules in F6.

Exam focus

The examining team has stated that the P6 exam will concentrate on the application of tax rules and will require the demonstration of evaluation and explanation skills.

They will set questions involving:

- the interaction of taxes
- decision making within the facts of a given situation
- making choices in a given situation and evaluating the tax savings which can be made.

Questions in section A will be open ended and are likely to require presentation in the form of a report or letter.

Section B questions will be more structured in their requirements.

paper P6

Aim of the paper

To apply relevant knowledge and skills and exercise professional judgement in providing relevant information and advice to individuals and businesses on the impact of the major taxes on financial decisions and situations.

Main capabilities

- Understanding of the tax system through the study of more advanced topics within the taxes studied previously and the study of stamp taxes (A)

- Impact of relevant taxes on various situations and courses of action, including the interaction of taxes (B)

- Minimising and/or deferring tax liabilities by the use of standard tax planning measures (C)

- Communication with clients, H M Revenue and Customs and other professionals in an appropriate manner (D)

The keys to success: Paper P6

Master the technical content

- Learn the rules, definitions and pro formas
- Practise questions to improve your ability to apply the techniques and perform the calculations
- Practise writing explanations of the rules to improve your understanding and written skills
- Be prepared to produce a report /letter / memorandum.

Provide advice and exercise judgement – Higher skills

- Express yourself in clear, concise technical language.
- Apply common sense to the problem as well as your technical knowledge.
- Tailor your answer to the facts of the question and make references to the scenario given.
- Be prepared to express an opinion or draw a conclusion from the facts given – if the question asks for an opinion, give one.
- Be prepared to suggest improvements to a proposed strategy and to identify tax planning opportunities.
- When dealing with more than one tax, address each one separately.

chapter 1

Income tax – overview and investment income

In this chapter

- Income tax pro forma.
- Rates of income tax.
- Married couples and civil partners.
- Child benefit tax charge.
- Exempt income.
- Property income.
- Rent-a-room relief.
- Furnished holiday accommodation.
- Real estate investment trusts.
- Effective rate of tax payable on dividends.

Income tax – overview and investment income

Exam focus

The computation of income tax is likely to feature throughout the exam.

Income from property is another key topic covered in this chapter.

It is also important to understand the marginal effect of transactions (i.e. the additional income tax payable as a result of receiving additional income, or the income tax savings where income is reduced).

Exam focus

The income tax computation is essential knowledge.

Use the following pro forma to gain easy marks on this aspect of the exam.

Income tax pro forma

Income tax computation – 2015/16

	£
Total income	x
Less: Reliefs	(x)
Net income	x
Less: Personal allowance	(x)
Taxable income	x

Income tax – analyse income

	Other	Savings	Dividend
Basic rate band (first £31,785)	20%	20% (Note)	10%
Higher rate band (£31,786 – £150,000)	40%	40%	32.5%
Additional rate band (over £150,000)	45%	45%	37.5%

Chapter 1

Income tax payable

	£
Total income tax (per rates)	x
Less: Tax reducers	(x)
Income tax liability	x
Less: Notional tax credit on dividends	(x)
Real tax credits/PAYE	(x)
Payments on account	(x)
Income tax payable/(repayable)	x/(x)

Notes:

(1) If savings income falls into the first £5,000 of taxable income it is taxed at 0% (not 20%).

(2) Foreign dividends assessed on a remittance basis for a higher rate or additional rate taxpayer will be taxed at 40% or 45% accordingly (not 32.5% or 37.5%).

Key Point

Extend the basic rate and higher rate bands if a taxpayer makes payments into a personal pension scheme.

Exam focus

Exam kit questions on this area:

- Mirtoon
- Dana
- Shuttelle
- Stella and Maris
- Ziti
- Kesme and Soba
- Cate and Ravi

Reliefs

- Interest on qualifying loans – paid gross
- Loss reliefs
- Maximum deduction from total income = greater of
  - £50,000
  - 25% x adjusted total income (ATI)
- Therefore the restriction will be £50,000 unless ATI exceeds £200,000.
- ATI is calculated as:

	£
Total income	X
Less: Gross PPCs	(X)
ATI	X

Exam focus

The maximum restriction is more likely to be examined in the context of loss relief (Chapter 13)

Personal allowance (PA)

- Available to all individuals
- £10,600 for 2015/16
- Deducted from net income to give taxable income
- Transferable amount £1,060 (see later)
- Lost if not used in the year

Chapter 1

Reduction of PA – higher rate taxpayers

- If ANI > £100,000:
  - reduce PA by:
    50% × (ANI – £100,000)
- If ANI > £121,200:
  - no PA
- Effective rate of tax on income between £100,000 to £121,200: 60%
- ANI is calculated as:

	£
Net income per IT comp	x
Less: Gross gift aid	(x)
Less: Gross PPCs	(x)
ANI	x

Exam focus

Exam kit questions on this area:

- Tetra
- Shuttle

Marriage Allowance

- A spouse or civil partner can elect to transfer a fixed amount of the PA to their spouse/civil partner.
- This is known as the marriage allowance (MA).
- Neither spouse/civil partner may be a higher or additional rate taxpayer.

Method:

- The fixed amount of PA to transfer:
  = 10% of the individual's PA
  = £1,060 for 2015/16.
- There is no provision for transferring less than this amount.
- Relief is given by reducing the recipient's income tax liability by a maximum of £212 (i.e. £1,060 x 20% BR income tax).

Income tax – overview and investment income

Tax reducers

- EIS, SEIS and VCT relief = 30%/50%/30%
- DTR = Lower of UK and overseas tax

Rates of income tax

- Income tax rate bands apply to the different types of income in the following order:
    1. other income
    2. savings income
    3. dividend income
- To maximise tax relief offset PA and reliefs against income in the same order as above.

Income

Other income:

Employment income
Trading income
Property income
Pension income
Trust income

Savings income:

- Interest received net of (20%) tax: bank, building society, unquoted loan stock issued by UK resident companies.
- Interest received gross: NS&I accounts, gilts, treasury stock, exchequer stock, quoted loan stock issued by UK resident companies.

Dividend income:

- Received net of deemed 10% tax.
- This includes foreign dividends for all UK resident individuals.

Married couples and civil partners

Joint income

- Applies to married couples and civil partnerships
- The income arising from assets (except shares in family companies) held jointly by husband and wife is normally split 50:50.
- An election is available to split the income according to beneficial ownership.
- The election cannot be made for joint bank or building society accounts.

Parental dispositions

- Income earned by a child from a parental disposition = taxed on the parent if the gross income received in the tax year exceeds £100 p.a.

Child benefit tax charge

A child benefit charge arises where:
- an individual receives child benefit, and
- they, or their spouse/civil partner, have ANI ≥ £50,000.

ANI = as for the restriction of the basic PA.

Income	Tax charge
£50,000 – £60,000	1% of child benefit for each £100 of income over £50,000
Over £60,000	The amount of child benefit received

Both the appropriate percentage and the tax charge are rounded down to the nearest whole number.

Where the charge applies the taxpayer must
- complete a tax return
- pay the charge through the self-assessment system.

The tax charge can be avoided by choosing not to claim child benefit.

Exempt income

- Interest on
  - (i) NS&I savings certificates
  - (ii) Save As You Earn (SAYE) share save accounts
  - (iii) Repayment interest (interest on tax repayments)
- Dividends received on shares from venture capital trusts (VCTs).
- Scholarships and educational grants.
- Prizes and winnings (i.e. premium bonds, betting).
- Statutory redundancy pay and the first £30,000 of compensation received for loss of employment.
- Certain state benefits (Child benefit, Universal credit).
- Income from individual savings accounts (ISAs).
- On death of a spouse/civil partner:
  - value of ISAs held at death = available as additional ISA allowance for surviving spouse/civil partner.

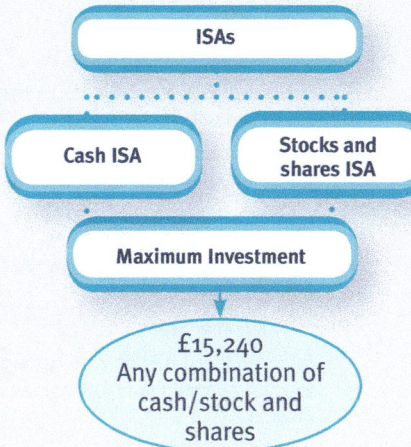

Property income

- Taxes income from land and property.
- Taxable income computed using trading income rules; accruals basis, wholly and exclusively test.
- Taxed as other income at:
  - 20%, 40% or 45%.
- Additional points re expenses:
  - interest paid = allowable deduction for individuals
  - 10% wear and tear allowance for furnished lettings can be claimed
  - for residential property, capital allowances are only available on equipment used for property maintenance.
- Property income losses
  - for individuals, can only be carried forward against future UK property income.

Pro forma – property income

	£
Rent receivable in the tax year	X
Plus: Rental income portion of short lease premiums received in tax year (see below)	A
Less: Allowable expenses	(X)
Profit or (loss)	X/(X)

Key Point

Always assume wear and tear allowance is claimed for furnished properties.

Chapter 1

Premium for granting short leases only

Income element is calculated as:

$$A = \text{Premium} \times \frac{51 - n}{50}$$

Where n = no. of years of lease

Rent-a-room relief

- Furnished room in a main domestic residence.
- Gross rents ≤ £4,250
  - exempt, unless elect for loss.
- Gross rents > £4,250
  - normal property income calculation
  - unless elect for excess over £4,250 to be taxed (with no deduction for expenses).

Exam focus

Exam kit questions on this area:
- Kesme and Soba

Furnished holiday accommodation (FHA)

- Assessed as property income but:
  - treat as arising from a single and separate trade
- Advantages:
  - business asset for CGT rollover relief, gift relief and entrepreneurs' relief
  - relevant earnings for pensions relief
  - capital allowances on all P&M, including furniture.
- Losses:
  - can only be set against profits from the same FHA business
  - UK FHA losses can only be set against UK FHA profits
  - EEA FHA losses can only be set against EEA FHA profits
  - firstly offset in the same year
  - then carry forward.

- Conditions:
  - situated in UK or EEA
  - let furnished on commercial basis
  - available to let $\geq$ 210 days/tax year
  - actually let $\geq$ 105 days/tax year
  - if own more than one property, averaging is available to satisfy the 105 day rule
  - not let for periods of 'long term occupation' (occupied by same person > 31 consecutive days) in excess of 155 days in a 12 month period.

Exam focus

Exam kit questions on this area:

- Monisha and Horner

Real estate investment trusts (REITs)

- Quoted property investment trust.
- Dividends received by individual from REIT:
  - treated as property income
  - received net of 20% tax.

Effective rate of tax payable on dividends

Income tax payable on cash dividend received:

- BR taxpayer (10% – 10%) = 0%
- HR taxpayer (32.5% – 10%) x 100/90 = 25%
- AR taxpayer (37.5% – 10%) x 100/90 = 30.555%

Income tax – overview and investment income

chapter 2

Employment income – income tax and national insurance

In this chapter

- Employment income – pro forma.
- Benefits summary.
- Vehicle benefits.
- Living accommodation.
- Beneficial loans.
- Use of assets.
- Gift of assets.
- Share options – tax treatment.
- Approved schemes.
- Employee shareholder shares.
- Lump sum payments.
- National insurance.

Employment income – income tax and national insurance

Exam focus

Employment is a particularly important area.

Skills required may vary from performing the basic calculation of employee benefits to higher skills. For example, making decisions between whether an employee should accept a company car or run their own car and take a cash alternative from the business instead.

You may also be required to express an opinion on whether an individual, given a particular scenario, is likely to be treated as self-employed or as an employee.

Employment income – pro forma

	£	£
Salary		x
Bonus/Commission		x
Benefits		x
Reimbursed expenses		x
Gross earnings		x
Less: Allowable expenses (See overleaf)		(x)
Add: Redundancy payment	x	
Less: Exempt portion (First £30,000 of non-contractual redundancy is tax free)	(x)	
		x
Employment income		x

Chapter 2

Exam focus

Exam kit questions on this area:

- Morice and Babine plc
- Jerome and Tricycle ltd
- Shuttelle
- Pita plc
- Cate and Ravi

Allowable expenses

- Contributions to employers registered occupational pension scheme.
- Subscriptions to professional bodies.
- Charitable donations under a payroll deduction scheme.
- Travel, subsistence and entertaining incurred wholly, exclusively and necessarily in the performance of the office or employment (see Note).
- Cost of partnership shares acquired in a share incentive plan (SIP).
- Deficit on mileage allowance (AMAP).

Note: Travel and related expenses

(i) Not travel from home to permanent workplace.

(ii) Travel from home to a temporary workplace is allowed if the placement is expected to last less than 2 years.

Benefits summary

All directors and employees	Exempt benefits
General rule: Assessed on cash value of benefit **Special rules**: Non-cash vouchers – cost to employer Accommodation – see below	• Job related accommodation • Subsidised canteen (unless part of salary sacrifice scheme) • Up to £4 per week towards additional household costs where the employee works from home • Occupational pension contributions • Workplace parking • Removal expenses ≤ £8,000 • Overnight subsistence • Mobile phone (one) • Workplace nurseries • Childcare vouchers ≤ £55/week (or £28 for HR or £25 for AR employees) • Annual party ≤ £150 per person per annum • Eye care tests • Cheap loans ≤ £10,000 • AMAPs • Recommended medical treatment assisting return to work (up to £500 per employee per tax year)
Earning at a rate of ≥ £8,500 p.a. and directors **General rule**: Assessed on cost to employer (marginal cost if 'inhouse' benefit) **Special rules**: Company cars/vans/fuel Beneficial loans Gift and use of assets Accommodation - See below	

Exam focus

Points frequently examined:

- employee contributions
  - deduct amounts paid in tax year from benefit
  - but note special rules for car: capital contributions (max £5,000) and fuel contributions (not allowable)
- where the benefit is wholly and exclusive for employment
  - calculate benefit and deduct expense claim
- benefits not available for part of year
  - time apportion.

Key Point

To determine if the £8,500 threshold applies:

- gross earnings including all benefits
- no deductions except
  - occupational pension scheme contributions
  - payroll deduction scheme donations to charity.

Employment income – income tax and national insurance

Approved mileage allowance payments (AMAPs)

If employee uses own car, van, motorcycle or bicycle for business purposes:

AMAPs = tax free

If mileage allowance received > AMAP:

Excess = assessable benefit

If mileage allowance received < AMAP:

Shortfall = allowable deduction from employment income

Passenger payments (if provided) for taking colleagues on same business trip:

- tax free if up to statutory limit (5p per passenger)
- no deduction for a shortfall.

Exam focus

- The AMAP rates for cars and vans will be provided in the tax rates and allowances (but not the passenger or other rates).

Exam focus

Exam kit questions on this area:

- Hysop Ltd
- Morice and Babine plc
- Jerome and Tricycle Ltd
- Shuttelle
- Spike
- Pita plc

Vehicle benefits

Where employer provides vehicle used for private purposes by employee.

VEHICLE BENEFITS

Car benefit

Basic car benefit:

List price $\times$ % $\times \frac{n}{12}$

- list price, including extras
- employee capital contribution deductible (max £5,000)
- benefit reduced if unavailable > 30 days
- benefit includes all running costs except private fuel
- n = number of months car available

Private fuel

£22,100 $\times$ % $\times \frac{n}{12}$

- % based on car percentage
- Employee contributions ignored unless reimburses private fuel in full

Van benefit

- £3,150 p.a. for use of van
- £594 p.a. for private fuel
- Time apportion if unavailable > 30 days

Appropriate %

The percentage used to calculate the car benefit depends on CO_2 emissions.

Emission rate per kilometre travelled ('Base level')	Percentage
95 grams (given in exam)	14% petrol
Increased by 1% for every extra 5 grams emitted	(max 37%)
3% supplement for diesel engines	(max 37%)

Low emission car reduced rates:
- CO_2 emission rate ≤ 50 g/km: 5% (petrol) or 8% (diesel)
- CO_2 emissions 51-75 g/km: 9% (petrol) or 12% (diesel)
- CO_2 emissions 16-94 g/km: 13% (petrol) or 16% (diesel)

Living accommodation

Benefit	Amount assessable	Job-related accommodation
Basic charge	Higher of: • Annual value • Rent paid by employer	Exempt
Expensive accommodation charge (where employer owns property and cost is > £75,000)	(Cost – £75,000) × ORI ORI = official rate of interest (provided in the exam)	Exempt
Ancillary services:	Only applies if employee earns at a rate of > £8,500 p.a.	
• Use of furniture	20% × market value when first provided	Same as for non-job related accommodation except: Maximum total benefit restricted to 10% of other employment income
• Living expenses (e.g. heating, electricity, decorating)	Cost to employer	
• Council tax	Cost to employer	No charge

Key Point

- Where the employer rents the accommodation there can never be an expensive accommodation charge.
- For the expensive accommodation charge:

  Cost = Acquisition cost of the property **plus** capital improvements up to the **start** of the tax year.

  If the property is occupied by the employee more than 6 years after it was acquired by the employer:

  – substitute the acquisition cost with the market value at the date the property was first occupied.

Job-related accommodation

Definition

Accommodation which is:

- necessary for proper performance of employee's duties, or
- provided for the better performance of duties and it is customary to provide such accommodation, or
- provided as part of special security arrangements because of a specific threat to the employee's security.

Exam focus

Exam kit questions on this area:

- Shuttelle

Beneficial loans

Where an interest free/subsidised loan made to employee:

	£
Capital (see below)	
x official rate of interest (ORI)	X
Less: Interest actually paid	(X)
Assessable benefit	X

- ORI = 3% for September 2016 to March 2017 exam sittings (given in tax tables)

- Two methods of computation of capital:

  - Average method:

    $$\frac{\text{Opening balance} + \text{Closing balance}}{2} = \text{average capital}$$

  - Precise method:
    calculated each month on balance outstanding

- Either taxpayer or HMRC can elect for precise method to be used

Exceptions

- No benefit if:
  - total loans outstanding at any time in the tax year is ≤ £10,000, or
  - loans made on ordinary commercial terms (i.e. same terms as to public)

Exam focus

- The benefit should be calculated using both methods in the exam unless the questions states otherwise

Use of assets

- Benefit:

  20% × MV when first made available

- 20% rule does not apply to private use of cars, vans and accommodation provided by employer

Gift of assets

New asset:

Benefit = cost to employer

Used asset:

- Benefit is greater of:

  Method 1

	£
– Market value at time of transfer	X
Less: Amount paid by employee	(X)
	X

  and

  Method 2

– Market value when first used	X
Less: Amount charged as benefit over period of use	(X)
Less: Amount paid by employee	(X)
	X

- These rules do not apply to transfer of:

  - a used car or van
  - bicycles provided for work.

  The benefit in this instance = Method 1

Share options – tax treatment

	Unapproved	**Approved**
Grant of option	No tax	No tax

Exercise of options (i.e. buy shares)	Income tax and NIC
	Collected under PAYE immediately
	Employment income charge:
	
	£
	MV @ exercise date x
	Less:
	  Cost of option (x)
	  Cost of shares (x)
	Employment income charge x
		No tax

Sale of shares	CGT £ Proceeds x Less: Cost of shares (x) Chargeable gain x Cost of shares = MV when exercised	CGT £ Proceeds x Less: Cost of shares (x) Chargeable gain x Cost of shares = Exercise price

Notes

(1) Class 1A NIC will be payable by the employer
   - unless the shares are quoted,
   - in which case class 1 will apply, which means the employee will also be liable.

(2) The gain is taxed at 0%, 10%, 18% or 28% depending on the availability of the AEA, entrepreneurs' relief and level of taxable income.

(3) Entrepreneurs' relief will only be available if
   - the employee owns at least 5% shareholding of the company
   - for the previous 12 months prior to sale.

   Except for EMI shares, where
   - the 12 months ownership commences at the date the option is granted, and
   - there is no 5% holding requirement.

Exam focus

Exam kit questions on this area:
- Spike

Approved schemes

Approved share option schemes

	CSOP	EMI	SAYE
Participation	Employer chooses	Employer chooses	All employees
Maximum value	£30,000 per employee	£250,000 per employee. Scheme max £3m	£500 per month
Exercise period	3 – 10 years	Up to 10 years	3 or 5 years
Issue price	MV	Issue at MV to avoid IT charge	Not < 80% of MV
Base cost of shares for CGT	Price paid	Price paid plus discount taxed as income on exercise (if any)	Price paid
Other	If own > 30% of company = excluded from the scheme	Gross assets ≤ £30m. Employees < 250. ER period of ownership runs from date of grant (not date shares acquired) and no need to own ≥ 5% of OSC	

Share incentive plan (SIP)

Participation	All employees
Awarded free shares	Max £3,600 per year
Purchase partnership shares	Max = lower of: • £1,800, and • 10% salary Cost = allowable deduction against employment income
Awarded matching shares	Max 2 per partnership share
Dividends	Tax free if invested in further shares

Holding period	• 5 years – IT and NIC free
	• If 3-5 years IT and NIC on lower of:
	  – initial value of the shares
	  – Value of the date of withdrawal
	• If 3 years
	  IT and NIC on value of the shares at the time when they cease to be held in the plan

Base cost of shares	MV when removed from plan

Employment income – income tax and national insurance

Exam focus

In the exam you may be required to recommend a suitable approved share scheme based on the facts in a particular situation.

Use the following factors to assist in deciding the most appropriate option:

- participants – open to all/selective scheme
- share award vs share option scheme
- financial limits – amount to be awarded
- size of company – EMI only available to smaller companies
- holding period for shares/options.

Exam focus

Exam kit questions on this area:

- Morice and Babine plc
- Flame plc Group
- Pita plc
- Klubb plc

Employee shareholder shares

- Employee shareholders give up certain employment rights, such as statutory redundancy pay and protection against unfair dismissal, in return for shares in their employer company.

To obtain tax relief:

- the awarded shares must be worth at least £2,000, and
- there must be no consideration paid for the shares other than the surrender of employment rights.

Tax relief

	Employee does not own a material interest (Note 1)	Employee owns a material interest
Income tax and NIC	Income tax charge: £ Value of shares awarded X Less: Tax free amount (Note 2) (2,000) Employment income X NIC charge: if shares readily convertible into cash	Income tax and NIC charges: full value of shares awarded - treated as employment income - taxable in the normal way.
Capital gains tax	On the disposal of the first £50,000 value of shares awarded (Note 3): - Chargeable gains arising = exempt - Losses arising = not allowable If employee owns ESS and other shares in the company: - can decide the proportion of shares disposed of that = treated as ESS	- no exemption available - disposal of shares = taxed in the normal way

Employment income – income tax and national insurance

Notes:

1. Material interest = own at least 25% of the voting rights.
2. Employee = deemed to have paid £2,000 for the shares.
3. First £50,000 shares eligible for the exemption = value at acquisition (not disposal).

Lump sum payments

- generally associated with termination
- but may be used as an incentive to attract an employee

Three types:

Wholly exempt	Fully taxable	First £30,000 exempt
• Payments for death, injury and disability • Statutory redundancy pay • Approved lump sum on retirement	• Pay in lieu of notice where contractual • Reward for past or future services	• Genuine ex-gratia compensation for loss of office (see below)

Termination payments on loss of office

- If contractual = taxable
- If non-contractual / ex-gratia = first £30,000 exempt
  - £30,000 includes statutory redundancy pay
- Restrictive covenants (i.e. restraint of trade) = fully taxable

Taxable amounts

- Assessed in year of receipt
- Paid before P45 = Paid net of PAYE
- Paid after P45 = Paid net of marginal rate income tax
- Taxed as top slice of income (after dividends).

Exam focus

Exam kit questions on this area:
- Tetra
- Pita plc

National insurance

Employees

Class 1 primary

- Employees pay class 1 primary NICs on their 'cash earnings'.
- Cash earnings includes:
  - any remuneration derived from employment and paid in money
  - vouchers exchangeable for cash or goods
  - reimbursement of cost of travel between home and work.
- Cash earnings does not include:
  - exempt employment benefits
  - most non-cash benefits
  - reimbursement of business expenses.
  - mileage allowance ≤ 45p per mile.
- Payable by all employees
  - aged 16 to state pension age
  - Note: an upper age limit applies.
- Payable at 12% on earnings between £8,060 and £42,385.
  - Note: an upper limit applies to the 12% rate.
- Payable at 2% on earnings above £42,385.
- Contributions are collected by the employer through the PAYE scheme.

Employers

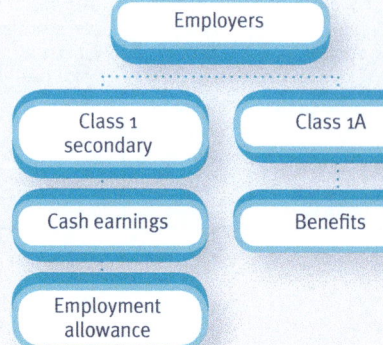

Class 1 secondary

- Cost borne by employer.
- Allowable trading expense for tax purposes.
- Rate of 13.8% on earnings over £8,112 per annum.
  - Note: no upper limit.
- Paid on 'cash earnings', as for class 1 primary.
- Paid in respect of employees aged ≥ 16.
  - Note: no upper limit.
- Employment allowance available.
- Payable with class 1 primary contributions through PAYE system.
- Payable on 22nd of the next month (electronic payments), or 19th of the next month if not paid electronically.

Employment allowance

- Up to £2,000 p.a. allowance.
- Deducted from class 1 secondary NICs only.
- Claimed though the RTI PAYE system.

Class 1A

- Payable by the employer only.
- Rate of 13.8% on assessable benefits provided to the employee.
- Payable by 22 July following the tax year if paid electronically) or 19 July (if not paid electronically).

Key Point

Where benefits are provided to employees earning < £8,500 p.a.:

- no class 1A NICs are payable.

Employment income – income tax and national insurance

chapter 3

Relief for pensions

In this chapter

- Pensions – overview.
- Types of registered pension schemes.
- Tax relief.
- Annual allowance.
- Lifetime allowance.
- Benefits on retirement.

Relief for pensions

Exam focus

Individuals investing in a registered pension scheme can reduce their income tax liability at their highest marginal rate in the tax year in which they make the investment.

Questions may require you to:

- provide information regarding the rules about the maximum amount a person is permitted to invest in their pension scheme
- advise a client as to how much tax they can save if they invest in a registered pension scheme, and/or
- advise a client as to the maximum amount they should invest in a particular tax year in order to maximise their tax relief.

Pensions – overview

- Tax relief available for contributions by under 75 year olds into HMRC registered pension schemes.
- Scheme must satisfy conditions.
- Must not invest in prohibited assets:
  - residential property
  - personal chattels
  - private investment assets (e.g. fine wine, art, classic cars, antiques).

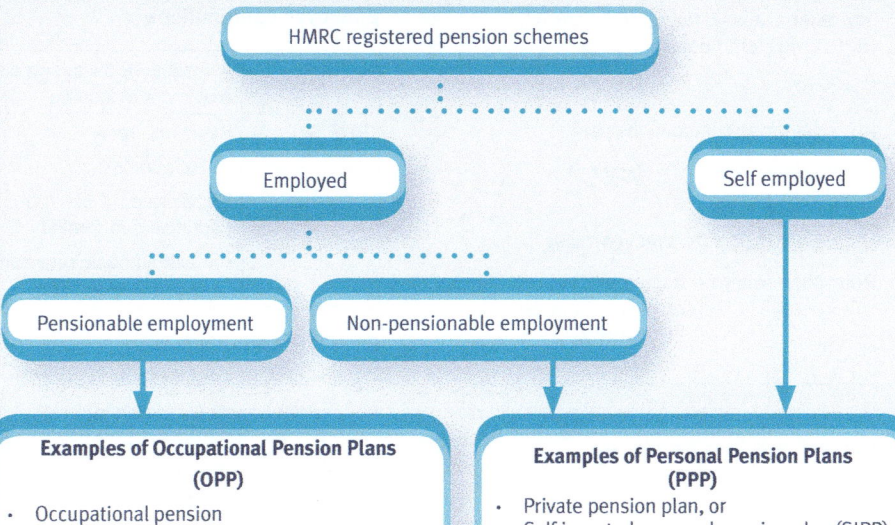

Relief for pensions

Tax relief

Tax relief available for contributions into HMRC registered pensions of up to:

Lower of:

(a) Total gross contributions paid

(b) Maximum amount = Higher of:

   (i) £3,600
   (ii) 100% × (relevant earnings).

Relevant earnings = trading profits, employment income, FHL income.

Exam focus

Exam kit questions on this area:

- Tetra
- Shuttelle
- Stella and Maris

Method of relief

Employee contributions

OPP	Allowable deduction against employment income
PPP	Basic rate relief • at source Higher rate / additional rate relief • extend basic rate band / higher rate band

Employer contributions

- tax allowable against business profits
- exempt benefit for individual
- taken into account when calculating total contributions to be compared with the annual allowance (AA).

Annual allowance (AA)

- Where total contributions paid into pension schemes > the current year AA of £40,000 plus unused AA b/f:
  - a tax charge arises on the excess.
- The tax charge is:
  - taxed as the individual's top slice of income.
  - paid through the self-assessment system.

- Unused AA b/f from the **previous three tax years** is taken into account:
  - can only be c/f if the individual was a member of a registered pension scheme for that tax year
- The AA limit for 3 years prior to 2015/16 was:
  - 2014/15: £40,000
  - 2013/14: £50,000
  - 2012/13: £50,000
- Order of utilisation:
  - current year AA is used first
  - then earlier three years unused amount, on a FIFO basis

Exam focus

In the examination:

- add the excess to the taxpayer's total income, and
- tax that part last (i.e. after dividends).

Exam focus

Exam kit questions on this area:

- Shuttelle
- Stella and Maris

Relief for pensions

Lifetime allowance (LA)

- LA = Total pension value that can obtain tax relief
- LA can not exceed £1,250,000.
- Considered when individual becomes entitled to take his pension/lump sum on retirement.
- If the value of the pension fund at the time exceeds the LA: an additional charge arises.

Benefits on retirement

Pension fund grows tax-free

- Exempt income tax.
- Exempt capital gains tax.

Commencement of benefits

- Aged 55.
- Can continue to work and draw a pension.

Tax free lump sum

- Maximum = 25% of lower of
  (1) value of fund
  (2) lifetime allowance (LA).

- The balance of the fund can be withdrawn at any time.
- Withdrawals from the balance are subject to income tax at normal rates (20%, 40% or 45%).

If value of fund > LA:

- Income tax charge on excess
  - at 25% if used to purchase a pension
  - at 55% if taken as a lump sum.

Pension income

- Pension income = taxable earned income.
- On death – pension income and/or lump sums for dependants may be made.

chapter 4

Capital gains tax – introduction

In this chapter

- Scope of CGT.
- CGT computation procedure – individuals.
- Pro forma CGT computation.
- Chargeable gain computation – individuals.
- Part disposals.
- Chattels.
- Assignment of leases.
- Capital losses.
- Connected persons.
- Married couples and civil partners.
- Payment by instalments.

Capital gains tax – introduction

Exam focus

Evaluating capital gains and losses are likely to feature heavily in the exam.

Questions are likely to feature both computational and planning aspects.

This chapter provides the tools to enable you to deal with the computational aspects of different scenarios.

Scope of CGT

- A chargeable gain arises when
  - a chargeable disposal is made
  - by a chargeable person
  - of a chargeable asset.
- Companies
  - pay corporation tax.
- Individuals
  - pay capital gains tax.

Scope of CGT

Chargeable persons
- individual
- company
- trustee
- partners in a partnership

Chargeable assets
- all assets unless specifically exempt

Chargeable disposals
- sale/gift of whole/part of asset
- loss/destruction of asset
- compensation for damage
- capital sums received re surrender of rights

Exempt assets
- gains – no CGT
- losses – no relief
- examples:
  - qualifying corporate bonds (QCBs)
  - gilts
  - trading inventory
  - receivables
  - equity ISA investments
  - cash
  - endowment policy proceeds
  - motor cars
  - wasting chattels (e.g. horses, boats)
  - shares in VCT

Exempt disposals
- trading disposal
- transfers on death
- gifts to charity

CGT computation procedure – individuals

Compute the CGT payable by an individual for a tax year as follows:

(1) Calculate the chargeable gains / allowable losses on the disposal of each chargeable asset separately

(2) Consider availability of any CGT reliefs (Chapter 6)

(3) Calculate the net chargeable gains arising in the tax year

= (chargeable gains less allowable losses)

(4) Deduct capital losses brought forward

(5) Deduct the annual exempt amount (AEA) = taxable gains

(6) Calculate the CGT payable at 10%, 18% and/or 28% depending on the availability of entrepreneurs' relief (ER) and level of taxable income.

Pro forma CGT computation

	£
Net chargeable gains for tax year (after specific reliefs)	X
Less: Capital losses b/f	(X)
	X
Less: AEA (2015/16)	(11,100)
Taxable gains	X
CGT payable (10%, 18% and/or 28%)	X

Due date 31 January 2017
(31 January after end of tax year)

Payable by instalments may be possible (see later).

Chargeable gain computation – individuals

Exam focus

The following pro forma can be used as the basic layout for the computation of the chargeable gain/allowable loss arising on each disposal by an individual.

Elements of the pro forma are computed differently for specific assets (e.g. part disposals). The approach to take for assets with additional rules is shown on the subsequent pages.

	£
Consideration (a), (b)	X
Less: Incidental costs of sale (c)	(X)
Net disposal proceeds	X
Less: Allowable expenditure	
– acquisition cost (d)	(X)
– incidental costs of acquisition (c)	(X)
– enhancement expenditure	(X)
Chargeable gain/loss	X/(X)

If a chargeable gain arises:

Chargeable gain before reliefs	X
Less: CGT reliefs (e)	(X)
Chargeable gain after reliefs	X

If an allowable loss arises:

Deduct any capital losses for the year from chargeable gains and include the net chargeable gains in the pro forma CGT payable computation.

Notes

(a) Disposal proceeds or market value (MV).

(b) Date of disposal:
date of contract/date conditions satisfied for conditional contracts.

(c) Legal expenses, valuation fees, advertising costs, stamp duty, auctioneer's fees.

(d) Cost/MV/probate value.

(e) Gift relief, rollover relief, incorporation relief, PPR and letting relief, EIS/SEIS relief.

(f) The gain is aggregated with other gains and losses and taxed at 0%, 10%, 18% or 28% depending on the AEA, ER and the level of taxable income.

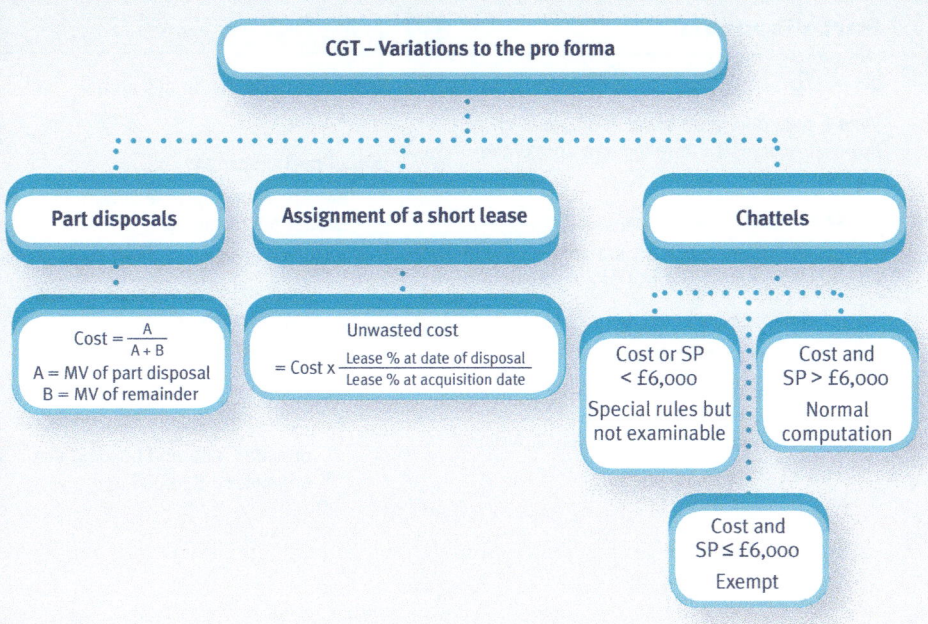

Capital gains tax – introduction

Part disposals

Key Point

Where only part of an asset is disposed of the cost is adjusted to reflect the cost of the part sold.

- Cost of part of asset disposed of:

  $\text{Cost} \times \dfrac{A}{A+B}$ A = consideration
  B = MV of the remainder

- incidental costs which relate:
  - wholly to the part sold
    = fully deductible
  - to the whole assest
    = apportioned as above (i.e. A/A+B)

Exam focus

Exam kit questions on this area:

- Kantar

Small part disposals

- elect to deduct proceeds from the base cost of part retained
- applies if proceeds of part disposed of:
  - ≤ 5% of value of whole at date of part disposal, or
  - ≤ £3,000
- for land and buildings the limit is:
  - 20% of the value of the asset,
  - provided land and building sales do not exceed £20,000 in the year.

Chattels

Definition

Tangible movable property
(e.g. painting, jewellery, racehorse, boat, caravan).

Wasting chattels:

- expected life ≤ 50 years
  (e.g. racehorse, boat, caravan)
- exempt from CGT unless plant and machinery on which capital allowances available.

Non-wasting chattels:

- expected life > 50 years
  (e.g. antiques, painting)
- subject to £6,000 rule but special rules not examinable.

Assignment of leases

Long lease (i.e. > 50 years)	Short lease (i.e. ≤ 50 years)
• subject to normal CGT computation	• subject to special CGT computation • cost adjusted to reflect depreciating nature of the asset: $$\text{Allowable cost} \times \frac{\text{Percentage for remaining life on disposal}}{\text{Percentage for remaining life on acquisition}}$$ The % will be provided in the examination

Exam focus

Exam kit questions on this area:

- Ash

Capital losses

- Current year losses:
  - must be offset against gains if possible
  - cannot be restricted to preserve the AEA
  - carry forward remaining losses.
- Brought forward losses:
  - offset after current year losses
  - but net chargeable gains must not be reduced below the AEA.
- Losses in the year of death:
  - can be carried back 3 years
  - LIFO basis
  - can restrict to preserve AEA.

Connected persons

- Consideration for disposal = market value.
- Loss on disposal can only be offset against gains to same connected person.

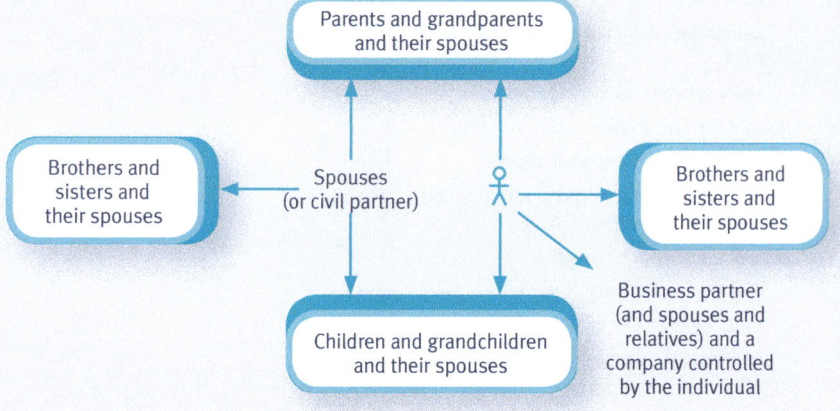

Civil partner and their relatives (as above) are also connected persons.

Married couples and civil partners

Exam focus

Scenarios involving married couples / civil partners are likely to be examined.

It is important that you know how to deal with transactions between spouses / civil partners and also to be able to suggest simple tax planning opportunities to enable them to minimise their total tax liabilities (see Chapter 12).

Exam focus

Exam kit questions on this area:

- Monisha and Horner

For CGT purposes, spouse / civil partner transfers are treated as follows:

- The connected persons rules are overridden.
- Spouse or civil partner transfers:
  - take place at nil gain/nil loss
  - regardless of any actual consideration which may have been received
- These rules only apply whilst the couple are living together (i.e. not separated).
- The transferor is deemed to dispose of the asset at its acquisition cost
  - i.e. the spouse/civil partner takes over the asset at its original cost.

Payment by instalments

Event	Payment details
Disposal proceeds received over a period >18 months	Instalments spread over shorter of: • 8 years • Period over which disposal proceeds received Instalments are interest free (unless late)
Gifts of: • Land or an interest in land • Shares or securities from controlling interest • Shares in unquoted company **Only** if gift relief not available	Pay by 10 equal annual instalments Starting on normal due date Instalments are interest bearing

Exam focus

Exam kit questions on this area:
- Cuthbert

chapter 5

Capital gains tax – shares and securities

In this chapter

- Share valuation rules.
- Matching rules – individuals.
- The share pool.
- Sale of rights (nil paid).
- Takeovers and mergers.
- QCBs and government securities.
- Liquidations.
- Losses on unquoted shares.

Share valuation rules

Transaction:	Consideration:
Sale	Sale proceeds
Gift	Market value
Transfer to a connected person	Market value

Market value of quoted shares:

Value = the mid- price quoted on the Stock Exchange

- i.e. the average of the lowest and highest prices on the disposal date

Unquoted shares

- No readily available price – professional valuation required.
- In the exam the value will be given.

Matching rules – individuals

Apply where an individual has made more than one purchase of shares of the same class in the same company.

Disposals matched with:

1. Acquisitions on same day.
2. Acquisitions in the next 30 days (FIFO basis).
3. The share pool (shares acquired before the date of disposal are pooled together

Exam focus

For the P6 exam, a thorough understanding of the basic share identification rules is required.

Disposal of shares by individuals

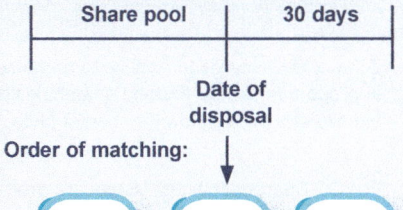

Method of computing gain:

Step 1 Determine the sale proceeds per share.

Step 2 Identify the date the shares are purchased and using the matching rules allocate the disposal to the time periods above.

Step 3 Compute the gains / losses arising on each matching rule.

The share pool

- The share pool contains shares in the same company, of the same class, purchased before the date of a disposal.
- It contains the amalgamated cost of shares acquired.
- The cost of shares disposed of is calculated as a proportion of the number of shares removed from the pool.
- If an individual disposes of shares:
  – in his personal trading company, and
  – is also an employee of that company:

  Entrepreneurs' relief (ER) is available (see Chapter 6).

Capital gains tax – shares and securities

Bonus issues

Definition

Distribution of free shares to shareholders based on their existing shareholding.

For CGT purposes bonus issues are treated as follows:
- The bonus shares are not treated as a separate holding of shares.
- The shares are treated as acquired on the same day as the original shares to which they relate.
- Therefore, the number of bonus shares are included in the share pool but at nil cost.

Rights issues

Definition

Offer of new shares to existing shareholders in proportion to their existing shareholding, usually at a price below the market price.

For CGT purposes rights issues are treated as follows:
- The rights shares are not treated as a separate holding of shares.
- The shares are treated as acquired on the same day as the original shares to which they relate.
- Therefore, the number of rights shares are included in the share pool, and the cost in the cost column in the same way as a normal purchase.

Sale of rights (nil paid)

Sales of rights (nil paid) = where shareholder does not take up rights issue and sells the 'right to buy' more shares.

The treatment of a 'sale of rights nil paid' for CGT purposes depends on the amount of sale proceeds (SP) received as follows:

If SP received are:	(i) > 5% of the value of the shares on which the rights are offered, **and** (ii) > £3,000.	(i) ≤ 5% of the value of the shares on which the rights are offered, **or** (ii) ≤ £3,000 if higher.
CGT treatment:	• deemed part disposal of original shares held. • normal part disposal computation required Where A = SP received B = MV of shares on which the rights are offered	• no chargeable disposal at the time of the sale of rights nil paid. • SP received are deducted from the cost of the original shares.

Takeovers and mergers

- Company (B) acquires shares in another company (A) by issuing shares to A's shareholders.
- 'Paper for paper' transaction = not a CGT disposal by A's shareholders. The new shares in B 'stand in shoes' of old A shares (i.e. take on the cost and acquisition date of A shares).
- Conditions:
  - clearance required from HMRC
  - B acquires > 25% of A's ordinary share capital (or a majority of the voting power of A).
  - the exchange is for bona fide commercial reasons and main purpose not the avoidance of tax.

With a share for share exchange, it is possible that:

- the old shares would qualify for ER if it were treated as a disposal
- but the new company is not the shareholder's personal trading company and so the later disposal of its shares would not qualify for relief.

However, the individual shareholder can:

- elect for the event to be treated as a disposal for CGT purposes, in which case the gain is taxed at 0%, 10%, 18% or 28% depending on the availability of the AEA, ER and level of taxable income.

If shares are sold for a mixture of cash and shares then a capital gain arises unless the cash element is small.

Chapter 5

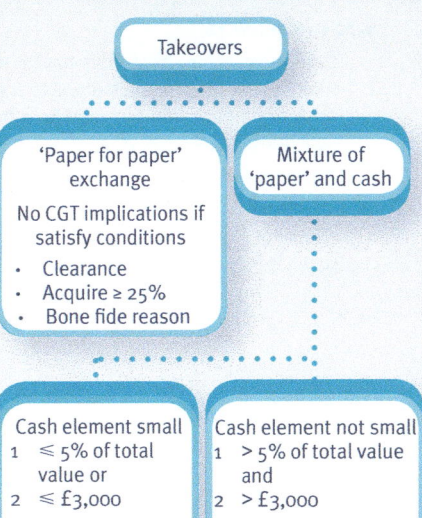

Part disposal of cash element:

Cost of asset sold =

Original cost $\times \dfrac{\text{Cash received}}{\text{Total consideration}}$

- Where consideration includes QCBs:
  - compute gain as if QCB was cash consideration
  - the frozen gain is charged when QCB sold.

Exam focus

Exam kit questions on this area:
- Banger Ltd and Candle Ltd
- Pescara

Capital gains tax – shares and securities

QCBs and government securities

- Exempt from CGT (i.e. no chargeable gain/no allowable loss).
- If ER is available on the gain at takeover the taxpayer must elect for ER and the gain will be taxed at 10% at takeover.
  - If ER is not claimed at takeover the frozen gain will be taxed at the appropriate rate in force when it crystallizes.

Definition

QCB: Normal commercial loan, expressed in sterling and not convertible into shares (e.g. company loan stock/loan notes).

Liquidations

- Shareholders are treated as having sold their shares for proceeds equal to the cash or other assets received from the liquidator.
- A chargeable gain or loss must be computed in the normal way.
- Consider pre-liquidation dividend payment.

Exam focus

Exam kits questions on this area:
- Banger Ltd and Candle Ltd

Losses on unquoted shares

- Capital losses are normally carried forward and offset against future capital gains.
- Can elect for a capital loss realised on the disposal of unquoted trading company shares to be treated as a trading loss.
- The capital loss can therefore be offset:
  - against income
  - of the tax year in which the loss arose, **and/or**
  - the preceding tax year.
- The shares must have been subscribed for, not purchased.

Capital gains tax – shares and securities

chapter

Capital gains tax – reliefs

In this chapter

- Overview of reliefs.
- Entrepreneurs' relief.
- Principal private residence relief.
- PPR – periods of occupation.
- Rollover relief.
- Reinvestment in depreciating assets.
- Gift relief.
- Incorporation relief.
- EIS reinvestment relief.
- SEIS reinvestment relief.

Capital gains tax – reliefs

Exam focus

CGT reliefs are an important aspect of CGT in practice.

Given the examining team's approach to examining real life practical situations they are likely to continue to feature regularly in exam questions.

You may be required not just to compute the reliefs but to state the conditions, when they apply and the tax implications.

Overview of reliefs

- After computing gains on disposals of individual assets consider the availability of reliefs.
- Some reliefs completely exempt a gain from CGT, or reduce the tax payable permanently, others only defer the gain to a later period.

Types of relief	
Permanent reliefs	**Deferral reliefs**
Entrepreneurs' relief	Rollover relief
PPR relief	Gift relief
Letting relief	Incorporation relief
SEIS reinvestment relief	EIS reinvestment relief

Entrepreneurs' relief (ER)

- Only available to individuals.
- First £10 million of gains on 'qualifying business disposals' are taxed at 10%, regardless of the taxpayer's income.
- Any gains above the £10 million limit = taxed in full at 18% / 28%.
- Gains qualifying for ER are set against any remaining basic rate band (BRB) before non-qualifying gains.
- The 10% CGT rate is calculated **after** the deduction of:
  - allowable losses, and
  - the AEA.
- Can choose to set losses and AEA against non-qualifying gains first to maximise relief.

  Exception:
  Any losses on assets forming part of the disposal of the business.

- Keep gains which qualify for ER separate from those which do not qualify.
- For 2015/16 disposals, the relief must be claimed by 31 January 2018.
- £10 million = a lifetime limit (partly used up each time a claim is made).

Capital gains tax – reliefs

Qualifying business disposals

The disposal of:

- the whole or part of an individual's trading business (i.e. sole trader or partner)
- assets of the individual's or partnership's trading business that has **now ceased**
- shares **provided**:
  - in the individual's 'personal trading company', **and**
  - the individual is an employee of the company (part time or full time).
- assets owned by the individual and used in their 'personal trading company' or trading partnership **provided**:
  - the individual also disposes of all or part of their partnership interest or shares in their personal trading company.
  - as part of their withdrawal of involvement in the partnership / company business.

An individual's 'personal trading company' is one where the individual:

- owns at least 5% of the ordinary shares
- which carry at least 5% of the voting rights.

When an individual disposes of goodwill to a close company (e.g. on incorporation) ER is not available in respect of the goodwill, unless the individual is a retiring partner.

Note that:

- "Part of a business"
  = a "substantial part" which is "capable of independent operation".
- Disposal of assets (i.e. not shares):
  Relief = not available on investment assets.
- No restriction to relief if company holds non-trading assets.
- No minimum working hours to satisfy employee condition.
- For approved EMI shares:
  no requirement to hold $\geq 5\%$ shareholding.

Key Point

The isolated disposal of an **individual business asset** used for the purposes of a continuing trade does **not** qualify.

Qualifying ownership period

- 12 months prior to the disposal, or
- Where a qualifying business is not disposed of but simply ceases:
  - relief will be available on gains on assets in use in the business at the time it ceased
  - where the assets are disposed of within 3 years of the date of cessation.
- For approved EMI shares:
  - qualifying period runs from the date the option is granted (not when shares acquired).

Capital gains tax – reliefs

Applying the relief

(1) Calculate the gains and losses on qualifying and non-qualifying assets separately.

(2) Net off losses relating to the qualifying business disposals against qualifying gains.

(3) Offset all other losses and the AEA against non-qualifying gains.

(4) If necessary deduct any remaining losses or AEA from the qualifying gains.

(5) Tax the gains as follows :
   – qualifying net chargeable gains at 10%
   – any non-qualifying net chargeable gains as normal at 18% or 28% (remember that qualifying gains utilise the BRB before non-qualifying gains).

Interaction of reliefs

- Other specific reliefs (if available) reduce chargeable gains before ER is considered.
- If also eligible for ER the remaining gain is taxable at 10%.

Exam focus

Exam kit questions on this area:
- Mirtoon
- Ash
- Farina and Lauda
- Ziti
- Jodie

Chapter 6

Principal private residence relief (PPR)

- Rules apply to house and garden (usually up to half a hectare)
- Owner occupied throughout
  - gain exempt
- Owner partly absent
  - PPR relief available

$$\text{Relief} = \text{Gain} \times \frac{\text{Periods of occupation}}{\text{Period of ownership}}$$

- If property let
  1. Calculate PPR relief
  2. Then give

     Letting relief:

     Lowest of:
     - (i) £40,000
     - (ii) PPR relief
     - (iii) Gain re letting

PPR – periods of occupation

- Actual occupation.
- Deemed occupation.

Exam focus

You may be presented with an individual's personal circumstances and be required to assess the period of ownership of a property which will qualify for PPR.

You should provide brief explanatory notes for periods of deemed occupation.

Capital gains tax – reliefs

Deemed occupation

Conditional	Unconditional

• Up to 3 years – any reason
• Any period – employed abroad
• Up to 4 years
  – working elsewhere in the UK (employed or self-employed)
  – working abroad if self-employed
• Must be actual occupation before and after
• Condition relaxed if reoccupation prevented by terms of employment
	• Last 18 months of ownership

Exam focus

Exam kit questions on this area:
- Mirtoon
- Kesme and Soba

Rollover relief (ROR)

- Relief for the replacement of qualifying business (QBAs).
- The gain arising on the disposal of a QBA can be deferred if proceeds reinvested in replacement QBAs within a qualifying period.
- Available to:
  - companies, individual sole traders, partnerships.

Exam focus

ROR is the only relief available to companies. It is therefore more often tested in a corporate situation.

Conditions

- Qualifying business assets
  - land and buildings
  - fixed plant and machinery
  - goodwill (unincorporated businesses only).
- Qualifying period
  - from 1 year before
  - to 3 years after the date of disposal.
- Claim is made
  - within 4 years from the later of the end of the tax year of:
    - sale, and
    - replacement
- For a 2015/16 disposal and replacement:
  - by 5 April 2020.

Capital gains tax – reliefs

Effect of relief

Where all proceeds are reinvested:

- The full gain on the old asset is 'rolled over' against the capital gains cost of the new asset.
- No tax is payable when old asset sold.
- Gain deferred until the new asset sold.

Deferred gain is:

- deducted from the base cost of the replacement asset, and
- deferred until the subsequent disposal of the replacement asset.

Partial reinvestment of proceeds

Where all proceeds are **not** reinvested:

- The gain that can be rolled over (i.e. deferred) is restricted (i.e. not all of the gain can be deferred).
- A chargeable gain arises
  = **lower** of
  – the proceeds not reinvested
  – the chargeable gain
- Taxable on the disposal of the original asset.
- The remaining gain is deferred.

Procedure for calculating ROR

1. Calculate the gain on disposal of the trade asset
2. Determine whether all sales proceeds have been reinvested in qualifying assets

Proceeds fully reinvested	Proceeds not fully reinvested
No gain now	Gain now = Lower of: (i) total gain (B) (ii) proceeds not reinvested (C)
Gain rolled over A	Gain rolled over (D): D = B – C

CGT base cost of new asset:
Cost   X
Gain rolled over (A)
               XX
	CGT base cost new asset:
	Cost X
	Gain rolled over (D)
	               XX

Interaction with entrepreneurs' relief

- ER is only available if the entire business is being sold.

  There is no ER on the disposal of an individual asset.

- If the entire business is sold and all the proceeds are reinvested into new qualifying assets:
  - consider ROR before ER
  - the gains may be deferred
  - ER only considered on subsequent disposal of replacement asset
  - based on conditions being satisfied at that time.

- If partial reinvestment and some gain remains chargeable now:
  - will be taxed at 0%, 10%, 18% or 28% depending on the availability of the AEA, ER and level of taxable income.
  - conditions for ER considered now.

Capital gains tax – reliefs

Exam focus

Exam kit questions on this area:

- Flame plc Group
- Liza

Reinvestment in depreciating assets

Definition

Depreciating asset (DA)

- life of $\leq$ 60 years

Common examples in exam:

- Fixed P&M
- Leasehold property of $\leq$ 60 years.

Method of relief

- Conditions and calculation of amount of relief = same as for ROR.
- Method of deferral = different.
- Gain not deducted from base cost of new asset.
- Gain is 'frozen' (i.e. deferred) and crystallises on the earliest of:
  - sale of DA
  - date DA ceases to be used in trade
  - 10 years from acquisition of DA.
- When deferred gain crystallises:
  - taxed at appropriate rate of CGT at that time (not at the time of deferral).

- Can defer a gain:
  - using a depreciating asset (for up to 10 years), and
  - later acquire a non-depreciating asset, and
  - claim to rollover the deferred gain instead (i.e. defer indefinitely until the replacement non-depreciating asset is sold)
  - provided the deferred gain has not previously become chargeable.

Exam focus

Exam kit questions on this area:

- Flame plc Group
- Bamburg Ltd
- Hyssop Ltd

Capital gains tax – reliefs

Gift relief (GR)

The gain arising on a gift is computed by using the market value of the asset.

GR must then be considered.

Recipient
Individual, trustee or company R in UK at time of gift

Applies to
Gifts and Sales at undervalue by individuals and trustees (not companies)

Effect
Deemed consideration = MV
Gain deferred against base cost to donee.

Individual donor

Qualifying assets
(1) Assets used in trade of donor or by his personal trading company (i.e. owns ≥ 5% voting rights)
(2) Shares in unquoted trading company
(3) Shares in donor's personal trading company
(4) Any asset where there is an immediate charge to IHT (e.g. gift into trust)
(5) Agricultural property eligible for APR

Asset not wholly used for business
Only gain related to trade use is deferred.
For shares (if own ≥ 5% voting rights) proportion of gain qualifying for relief is:

$$\frac{\text{MV Chargeable business assets}}{\text{MV Chargeable assets}}$$

Key Point

Restriction of (CBA/CA) only applies where donor holds ≥ 5% of shares.

If donor holds < 5% of shares:

- unquoted = no restrictions to GR
- quoted = no GR

Sale at undervaluation

Where the asset is sold, but for less than MV, the 'actual consideration' received is ignored:

- The gain is still calculated using MV.

If the actual consideration > transferor's cost:

- the excess is immediately chargeable
- the remaining gain can be deferred.

The chargeable gain arising now will be:

- taxed on the donor at either 0%, 10%, 18% or 28%
- depending on the availability of the AEA, ER or the level of taxable income.

If the actual consideration ≤ donor's cost:

- full gift relief available
- all chargeable gain deferred.

The deferred gain is taxed on the donee later at the appropriate rate when they dispose of the asset.

Capital gains tax – reliefs

Emigration of donee

If within 6 yrs of gift the donee emigrates:

- the deferred gain crystallises on the donee
- on the day before emigration.

Effect of relief

Regardless of how the gain is calculated, the deferred gain is:

- deducted from the base cost of the donee, and
- deferred until the subsequent disposal of the asset by the donee.

When the gain crystallises:

- taxed at appropriate rate of CGT at that time (not at the time of deferral).

Election

For a gift in 2015/16, a joint election is required:

- signed by both the donor and donee
- by 5 April 2020.

If gift into a trust:

- only needs to be signed by the settlor.

Exam focus

Exam kit questions on this area:

- Surfe
- Una
- King
- Farina and Lauda
- Ziti

Interaction with entrepreneurs' relief

- If ER is applicable:
  - the donor may choose not to claim gift relief in order to crystallise a gain and claim ER now instead.
- This is advantageous if the donee will not qualify for the relief on their subsequent disposal. For example, if they would not satisfy the employment condition and/ or one-year ownership rule.

- If the individual disposes of shares in a personal trading company:
  - gift relief is available:
    - subject to the (CBA / CA) restriction above
    - regardless of whether the individual works for the company.
  - If a gain remains after gift relief (due to the CBA/CA restriction) then ER will also be available provided:
    - the individual works for the company, and
    - it has been the individual's personal trading company
    - for the 12 months prior to the disposal.

Capital gains tax – reliefs

Incorporation relief

- Where an individual incorporates his sole trader or partnership business:
  - chargeable gains arise on the MV of the individual assets transferred.
- Incorporation relief is a relief which
  - automatically applies
  - to defer the net chargeable gains arising on incorporation
  - provided certain conditions are met.

Key Point

Where consideration is wholly shares:
- No gain on incorporation.
- Gains deferred until the subsequent disposal of shares.

Where non-share consideration is received:
- a chargeable gain arises on incorporation
- taxed at 0%, 10%, 18% or 28% depending on the availability of the AEA, ER and level of taxable income.

Exam focus

Exam kit questions on this area:
- Farina and Lauda

Conditions	- All of the assets of the business (except cash) must be transferred.
	- The transfer must be of a business as a going concern.
	- The consideration received must be wholly or partly in shares.
Effect	- No gains arise on incorporation.
	- Gains are deferred against the acquisition cost of the shares.
Consideration not wholly in shares	- Gain eligible for deferral: $$\text{Gain} \times \frac{\text{Value of shares issued}}{\text{Total consideration}}$$
	- Immediate gain in respect of non-share consideration which is taxed at 10% (if ER claimed) or 18% and 28%: $$\text{Gain} \times \frac{\text{Value of non-shares consideration}}{\text{Total consideration}}$$
Future disposal of shares	- On a later sale of the shares, the gain will normally qualify for ER provided conditions satisfied.

Capital gains tax – reliefs

Election to disapply	- Can elect for incorporation relief not to apply.
	- Gains on the assets transferred to the company would be taxed at 0%, 10%, 18% or 28% depending on the availability of the AEA, ER and level of taxable income.
	- No gains would be deferred against the cost of the shares, making the gain on their subsequent disposal lower.
	- May be beneficial to elect to disapply if:
	– gains covered by AEA, or
	– shares are to be sold shortly after incorporation (i.e within 12 months) so would not be eligible for ER.
	- Must elect within 2 years from 31 January following the end of the tax year in which the business is transferred.
	- For 2015/16 by 31 January 2019.

Planning points

- Must transfer all assets
  - may wish to retain property with large growth potential to avoid double charge to tax
  - consider gift relief as an alternative to transfer selected assets
  - as goodwill transferred to a related close company is not eligible for ER, it could be efficient to defer the gains under incorporation relief. When the gain becomes chargeable on disposal of the shares, ER can be claimed provided the share disposal qualifies.
- Defers gains pre ER
  - consider electing to disapply incorporation relief if likely to sell shares within 12 months.

Exam focus

Questions involving incorporation may require detailed knowledge of incorporation relief, gift relief and entrepreneurs' relief.

Capital gains tax – reliefs

EIS reinvestment relief

- Individual:
  - disposes of any asset
  - subscribes for qualifying shares in EIS scheme
  - between 1 year before and 3 years after gain
- Relief is lowest of:
  (1) the gain
  (2) amount subscribed for EIS shares
  (3) any smaller amount chosen
- Individual must be resident in UK when gain realised and on reinvestment
- Gain deferred until:
  - the disposal of the EIS shares by the investor, spouse / civil partner, or
  - the investor or spouse / civil partner (after a previous NGNL transfer) becomes non-UK resident (e.g. emigrates abroad) within 3 years of the issue of shares
- Claim within 5 years from 31 January following the end of the tax year in which the disposal occurred
- For 2015/16 disposals by 31 January 2022.
- Planning point:
  - choose to claim an amount of relief so that remaining gain is equal to the AEA and any available losses.
  - work backwards in CGT pro forma to calculate amount of claim required.

If the asset qualifies for ER a claim can be made such that gain is taxed in the year of disposal at 10%.

If a claim is not made the gain deferred will be taxed at the appropriate rate in force when it becomes chargeable.

If a gain deferred was entitled to ER at the point of deferral, it will still be taxed at 10% when it becomes chargeable.

SEIS reinvestment relief

- If an individual:
  - disposes of any chargeable asset, and
  - reinvests in qualifying SEIS shares, which
  - qualify for SEIS income tax (IT) relief

  some of the gain arising = **exempt** CGT.

- Any remaining gain is taxable in the normal way.

- Maximum SEIS exemption

  = 50% of the lower of the

  (i) gain

  (ii) amount reinvested

  (**Maximum CGT exemption = £50,000** as maximum that can qualify for IT relief = £100,000).

- Relief = flexible, can claim any amount up to the maximum.

- Claim = same as EIS claim:

  For 2015/16 = by 31 January 2022.

- Planning point:
  - as for EIS relief: leave remaining gain equal to AEA and any available losses

Capital gains tax – reliefs

- Withdrawal of relief:
  - If the disposal within three years is:

	Not at arm's length	At arm's length
IT relief withdrawn	All	Lower of: • All • (50% x SP received)
CGT relief withdrawn	All	$= \dfrac{\text{Amount of IT relief withdrawn (above)}}{\text{Original IT relief given}} \times \text{Gain}$

Exam focus

Exam Kit questions on this area:

- Pescara

Key Point

There is no reinvestment relief for VCT investments.

chapter 7

Stamp taxes

In this chapter

- Stamp duty and stamp duty land tax.

Stamp taxes

Exam focus

Stamp taxes may feature as part of a question, however a question will not be set exclusively on stamp taxes.

Stamp duty and stamp duty land tax

- Paid by purchaser.

Stamp Duty (SD) / Stamp Duty Reserve Tax (SDRT)	Stamp Duty Land Tax (SDLT)
Payable on	
• transfer shares/securities	• transactions in UK property
Rate	

• 0.5% of consideration
• SD only:
   – min £5
   – no charge if consideration ≤ £1,000
	• up to 12% depending on type of property (residential or commercial), and amount of consideration
	• rates given in tax rates and allowances

Specific exemptions	
Stamp Duty (SD) / **Stamp Duty Reserve Tax (SDRT)**	**Stamp Duty Land Tax (SDLT)**

• Exempt securities
  – government stock
  – most company loan stock (unless convertible)
  – unit trusts
  – AIM shares.	

General exemptions	

- Gifts
- Transfers of assets between 75% group companies
  - same definition as for 75% gains groups
  - not available if arrangements in force for purchasing company to leave group
  - SDLT exemption relief withdrawn if transferee company leaves group within 3 years of transfer, still owning the land.

Exam focus

Exam Kit questions on this area:

- Una
- Helm Ltd Group

chapter 8

Inheritance tax

In this chapter

- Charge to inheritance tax.
- Lifetime gifts.
- IHT computations.
- Due dates of payment.
- Valuation.
- Exemptions and reliefs.
- Death estate pro forma.
- Payment by instalments.
- Deed of variation.
- Married couples and civil partners.
- IHT and CGT on sales/gifts.
- Skipping a generation.

Inheritance tax

Exam focus

Inheritance tax regularly features in the P6 exam, often as part of a question involving other taxes too – particularly capital gains tax.

Charge to inheritance tax (IHT)

- Occasions of charge:
  - Lifetime gifts.
  - Death estate.
- Charged on:
  - a chargeable transfer (see later)
  - of chargeable property
  - by a chargeable person.
- Chargeable property:
  - all capital assets / wealth
  - no exempt assets for IHT.
- Chargeable person:
  - individuals.
- Gratuitous intent:
  - transfer must be a gift
  - intention to give asset away
  - not a poor business deal.

Lifetime gifts

- Two types:
  - Potentially Exempt Transfers (PETs)
  - Chargeable Lifetime Transfers (CLTs)

	PETs	CLTs	
Definition	Gift by individual to: • another individual • a disabled trust • certain old trusts (not examinable)	Gift which is not: • Exempt, or • a PET Main examples = gifts to trusts: • (except charitable trusts or those treated as PETs)	
Chargeable	Only if donor dies within 7 years of gift	At date of gift	Additional IHT if donor dies within 7 years of gift
Tax rates	Death rates	Lifetime rates	Death rates
Tax paid by	Donee	Donee, or Donor (gross up gift for tax paid)	Donee

Inheritance tax

IHT computations

Exam focus

An IHT charge can arise in 3 different situations. The computation in each situation is different and must be studied carefully.

1. Lifetime transfers – IHT on CLTs
2. Death – additional IHT on PETs and CLTs
3. Death estate

In each situation:

- Compute the chargeable transfer.
- Compute the taxable amount.
- Compute the tax.

The chargeable transfer

The first stage of the computation for each situation is always the same; compute the chargeable transfer:

	£	
Transfer of value:		
Value before	X	– Diminution in value principle
Value after	(X)	– Related property
	X	
Deduct:		
(1) Reliefs	(X)	– APR – BPR
(2) Exemptions	(X)	– (See later)
Chargeable transfer	A	

Order of using reliefs and exemptions – see later.

Chapter 8

Computing the taxable amount

Calculating the taxable amount is also the same for each situation. However, the calculation of the available nil rate band (NRB) differs.

	£
Chargeable transfer	A
Less:	
Available NRB	(X)
Taxable amount	X

Nil rate bands (NRB)

- For lifetime gifts – lifetime tax:
  - Use NRB in tax year of gift.
- For lifetime gifts – death tax:
  - Use NRB in tax year of death.
- For death estate:
  - Use NRB in tax year of death
- The NRBs will be provided in the tax rates and allowances.

Exam focus

Exam Kit questions in this area:
- Surfe
- Una
- Cuthbert
- Brad
- Pescara
- Farina and Lauda
- Ziti
- Kantar
- King

Inheritance tax

Computing the tax

1 – Lifetime tax on CLT

	£	£
Chargeable transfer (A)		222,000
Less:		
NRB at gift (say)	312,000	
Less: CLTs in 7 years prior to gift (say)	(170,000)	
NRB available		(142,000)
Taxable amount		80,000
IHT payable:		
(i) at 20% if donee pays tax		16,000
(ii) at 25% if donor pays tax		20,000

If donor pays tax:
Add IHT to value of chargeable transfer (A) to calculate gross chargeable amount (B)
i.e. (£222,000 + £20,000) = £242,000

Key Point

Note that the donor is primarily responsible for the lifetime tax due.

2 – Additional tax on lifetime transfers as a result of donor's death

Perform the following calculation for:

- each gift (CLTs and PETs) in the 7 years prior to death
- in chronological order

Gift 1 – CLT or PET

	£	£
Gross chargeable transfer (A or B)		365,000
Less:		
NRB at death	325,000	
Less: CLTs and chargeable PETs in 7 years prior to gift (1) (say)	(140,000)	
NRB available		(185,000)
Taxable amount		180,000

	£
IHT payable at 40%	72,000
Less: Taper relief (40%)(say)	(28,800)
Chargeable (60%)	43,200
Less: Lifetime tax paid (say)	(10,000)
IHT payable	33,200

Then perform the same calculation for Gift 2 etc.

Notes:

(a) Order of using reliefs and exemptions:

1. Exempt gifts, small, spouse, charity
2. APR
3. BPR
4. Fall in value
5. ME
6. AE current year, then b/fwd
7. Taper relief

Inheritance tax

(b) Taper relief

Years before death	% reduction
Over 3 but less than 4 years	20%
Over 4 but less than 5 years	40%
Over 5 but less than 6 years	60%
Over 6 but less than 7 years	80%

(c) Lifetime tax deduction:
 – cannot create a repayment of IHT.

3 – IHT on death estate

Death estate computation:

	£	£
Value of Estate		925,000
Less:		
NRB at death	325,000	
Less: CLTs and chargeable PETs in 7 years prior to death (say)	(180,000)	
NRB available		(145,000)
Taxable amount		780,000
IHT payable at 40%		312,000
Less: Quick succession relief		(X)
Double taxation relief		(X)
IHT payable		X

Due dates of payment

1. **Lifetime IHT**

Gift:	Due date:
6 April – 30 Sept	30 April in next year
1 Oct – 5 April	6 months after end of month of gift

2. **Additional IHT on lifetime gifts due to death**

   Due date – 6 months from end of month of death.

   Note: always paid by donee.

3. **IHT on death estate**

   Due date – 6 months from end of month of death.

   However, tax is required to be paid with delivery of accounts to HMRC, which may be earlier than due date.

Valuation

Exam focus

An exam question, particularly one involving the death estate, will also require you to value the assets being transferred.

1. **Gifts**

   - IHT uses the 'diminution in value' principle to calculate the 'transfer of value' (i.e. value by which the donor's estate has been reduced).

	£
Value of estate before tansfer	X
Less: Value of estate after transfer	(X)
Transfer of value	X

   - In most cases = value of asset gifted
   - In some cases the diminution in value > value of asset gifted.
     - e.g. gift of unquoted shares

Inheritance tax

Key Point

It is important to appreciate the difference here between CGT and IHT.

For CGT purposes the consideration used for a gift = valued at the market value of the asset gifted.

2 Related property

- Special rules where same type of property owned by:
  - Spouse/civil partner, or
  - Exempt body (e.g. charity) as a result of an exempt transfer to them by the donor or the donor's spouse/civil partner
- Applies when valuing a gift or an asset in an individual's estate

- Value of asset – 2 situations:

  (i) All assets except unquoted shares

  $$\frac{\text{Value of individual's share}}{\text{Value of individual's share} + \text{Related party share}} \times \text{Value of combined assets}$$

  (ii) Unquoted shares

  Use the same formula, but the 'number' of shares is used in the fraction, not the value.

Exam focus

The related property rules are often relevant in exam questions involving unquoted shares.

3 Other assets

General rule	Open Market Value
Quoted shares and securities	Lower of: 1/4 up rule and the average of the highest and lowest marked bargains.
Unquoted shares	No readily available market price – will vary depending on % holding. Value agreed with HMRC. In exam – value will normally be given.
Unit trusts	Lower bid price
UK freehold property	Jointly owned property: • Valuation ÷ number of joint owners. • Joint tenants – share passes automatically (not via will) to joint tenant. • Tenants in common – share inherited according to will. Value reduced by mortgage – unless endowment mortgage.
Life assurance	On own life = actual proceeds received • For benefit of named beneficiary under a declaration of trust – excluded from estate. • Any other life policy = higher of MV and premiums paid.

Inheritance tax

Exemptions and reliefs

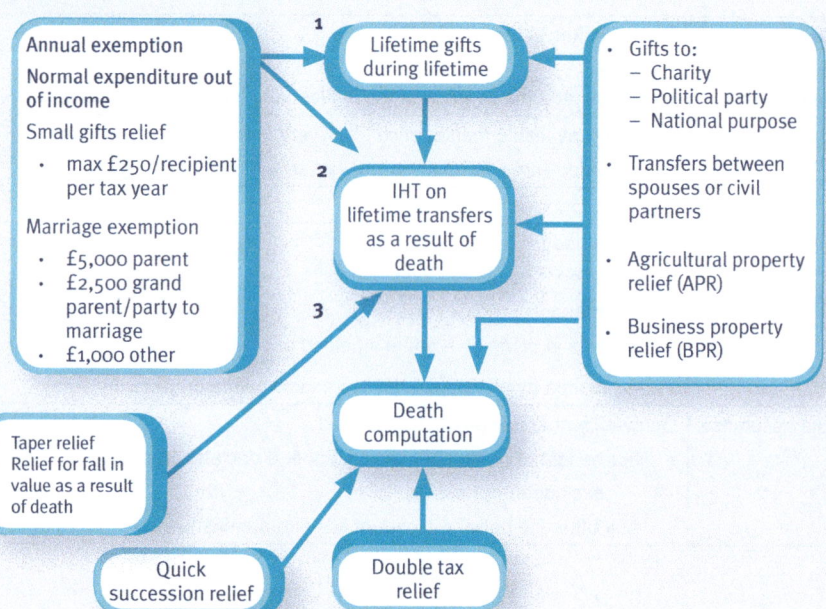

Key exemptions and reliefs

1 Annual exemption

- £3,000 per annum
- Applied to gifts in chronological order
- Used against PET – even if PET never becomes chargeable
- Unused amount can be carried forward one year
- Current year exemption used in priority to brought forward
- Applied after all other reliefs and exemptions have been applied.

2 Fall in value relief

- Applies in the calculation of death tax on PETs and CLTs.
- Donee must:
  - still own the asset at date of donor's death, or
  - have sold it in arm's length transaction.
- Deduct from chargeable amount the fall in value:
  - from: date of gift
  - to: date of death or earlier sale.
- Carry forward original chargeable amount.

Inheritance tax

Exam focus

Exemptions and reliefs will always feature in an IHT computation – it is important that you can identify when they are available and how they are applied.

Exam focus

Exam kit questions with exemptions and reliefs:

- Surfe
- Una
- Brad
- Cuthbert
- Farina and Lauda
- Pescara
- Ziti
- Kantar
- Stella and Maris

3 Business property relief (BPR)

Two key conditions:

- transfer of Relevant Business Property (RBP)
- Minimum period of ownership

Exam focus

This relief is extremely important and can be expected to feature in almost every exam.

- Applies to lifetime transfers and on death
- Applies to relevant business property

Relevant business property (RBP)

Property	Conditions	Relief
Quoted shares and securities	• Out of a controlling interest • Must be trading company	50%
Unquoted shares and securities	• Including AIM • Must be trading company • Only available on securities if have control based on shares	100%

Assets	• Land and buildings, P&M:
	  – Used by company controlled by donor, or
	  – Used by a partnership in which donor is a partner
		50%

Property	Conditions	Relief
Sole trader	• Unincorporated business or share in partnership • Must be the whole business not individual assets	100%

- Available on UK and overseas RBP.
- Not available on excepted assets (e.g. investments).
- Where company owns investments BPR is given on:

$$\text{Value of shares} \times \frac{\text{Company's business property}}{\text{Company's total assets (before liabilities)}}$$

Inheritance tax

Length of ownership

- Property must have been owned for ≥ 2 years (unless replacement property).
- Where business property was inherited and was eligible for BPR at that time:
  - there is no minimum ownership period for BPR on the second death (successive transfers rule).
- Where business property is transferred from a spouse/civil partner:
  - the combined length of ownership by the couple is considered.

Death tax on lifetime gifts

- Where additional IHT due on gift as a result of donor's death:
  - BPR only available where business property is still owned by the donee at the date of the donor's death.

Tax planning

- No IHT payable on assets which qualify for 100% BPR.
- No IHT saving from making lifetime gifts of assets which qualify for 100% BPR, better to gift on death.

Exam focus

Exam Kit questions on this area:

- Brad
- Ziti

4 Agricultural Property Relief (APR)

- Applies to lifetime transfers and on death
- Applies to the **agricultural value** of relevant agricultural property
- Agricultural property
  = farmland, pastures and farm buildings
- Only available on agricultural property situated in UK or EEA
- Rate of relief = 100%

Exam focus

Exam Kit questions on this area:

- Una

Length of ownership

- Property must have been owned for:

Agricultural property farmed by:	Ownership
The owner	Two years
A tenant	Seven years

- Successive transfers and spouse/civil partner transfer rules as per BPR

Death tax on lifetime gifts

- Retention rules as per BPR

Tax planning

- No IHT saving from making lifetime gifts which qualify for APR, better to gift on death.

Inheritance tax

Death estate pro forma

	Notes	£	£
Freehold property		x	
Less: Mortgage	(a)	(x)	
			x
Foreign property		x	
Less: Expenses	(b)	(x)	
			x
All other assets owned by deceased			x
Debts due to deceased			x
Accrued income			x
			x
Less: Outstanding debts	(c)		(x)
			x
Less: Exempt legacies	(d)		(x)
			x
Settled property	(e)		x
Gift with reservation (GWR)	(f)		x
Chargeable estate			x

IHT payable computation

	£	£
Chargeable estate		x
NRB at death	325,000	
Less: GCT's in previous 7 years	(x)	
NRB available		(x)
Taxable estate		x
IHT on taxable estate (40% or 36%)		x
Less: Quick succession relief		(x)
		A
Less: Double tax relief		(x)
Inheritance tax payable		B

Average estate rate (AER) = $\dfrac{A}{\text{Chargeable estate}} \times 100$

Due date:
Earlier of
- 6 months after the end of the month of death, o
- On delivery of the estate accounts
  (unless paid by instalments – see below)

Allocation of UK IHT payable:

- IHT payable on estate = apportioned at AER (after QSR)
- Tax paid by:

Settled property	Trustees
GWR	Recipient of gift
Remainder	
– overseas asset	Recipient of legacy (tax bearing gift)
– UK asset	Residual legatee (tax free gift)

Key Point

All assets are chargeable (i.e. no exempt assets for IHT at P6).

Assets that are exempt from CGT (e.g. Motor cars, gilts, ISAs, PPR etc) are not exempt from IHT.

Notes

(a) Repayment and interest-only mortgages and accrued interest. Do not deduct endowment mortgages. Deduct 10% of value if tenants in common.

(b) Expenses restricted to maximum 5% of foreign property value.

(c) Outstanding debts payable by the deceased (e.g. outstanding bills and other taxes due: IT, CGT, VAT).

(d) Exempt legacies = legacies to spouse, civil partner, charity, political party.

(e) Settled property = IPDI trust in where deceased is the life tenant (Chapter 10).

- Bring in the MV of the assets in the trust.

Inheritance tax

(f) Gifts with reservation = lifetime gift where donor retains a benefit (e.g. gift of legal title to house but donor still lives in it).
- Bring into estate computation as if gift never made
- can be avoided if donor pays market rate rent to donee.

Substantial legacies to charity

- Reduced rate of 36% applies to estates where:
  - total charitable legacies on death ≥ 10% x (baseline amount)
- Baseline amount
  = Taxable estate
    plus charitable legacies.
- Can use a Deed of Variation to increase a charitable legacy to benefit from the 36% rate.

Exam focus

Exam kit questions with a gift with reservation:
- Mirtoon
- Una
- Pescara

Quick Succession Relief (QSR)

- Look for gifts to the deceased in the five years before death
- Tax credit relief
- QSR = (IHT on first gift) x appropriate %
- IHT on first death = (estate rate on first death) x value of the legacy
- Percentages:

Years between deaths		Appropriate % to use in formula
More Than	Not more than	
0	1	100%
1	2	80%
2	3	60%
3	4	40%
4	5	20%

- Given before DTR

Double Tax Relief (DTR)

- Lower of
   (i) overseas tax suffered
   (ii) AER x (overseas property value brought into estate)

Inheritance tax

Payment by instalments

- Elect to pay in ten equal annual instalments.
- Only the following assets qualify:
  - land and buildings
  - unincorporated businesses
  - shares or securities where the donor has a controlling interest
  - some unquoted shares and securities (detail not examinable).
- Available on
  - death estate
  - PETs and CLTs which become chargeable on death, and
  - CLTs where the donee pays the tax.
- Land and buildings
  - instalments interest bearing.
- Other qualifying assets
  - instalments interest free.
- If asset sold in instalment period
  - outstanding balance must be paid immediately.

Exam focus

Exam questions on IHT will usually involve an element of planning, including advising on how a transfer of assets could be organised more effectively for IHT purposes (see Chapter 12).

Deed of variation

- To change the distribution of assets under will or intestacy.
- Conditions:
  - all beneficiaries must agree
  - must be in writing
  - must contain clause that it is to be effective for IHT purposes
  - made within 2 years of death.
- Situations when useful:
  - to skip a generation where children wealthy in own right.
  - to increase a charitable donation to benefit from the reduced 36% rate on death estate.

Married couples and civil partners

Exempt transfers

- Inter spouse / civil partner transfers = exempt
  - unlimited in amount
- Exception = if recipient spouse / civil partner is non-UK domiciled
  - maximum exemption = current NRB

Inheritance tax

Election to be treated as UK domiciled

- Non-UK domiciled spouse / civil partner
  - can elect to be treated as UK domiciled
  - irrevocable election
  - by individual in lifetime, or by executors within 2 years of death of individual
- Advantage = unlimited inter-spouse / civil partner exemption
- Disadvantage = subject to IHT on overseas assets

Transfer of unused nil rate band

- If the NRB has not been utilised at the time of a person's death, the proportion of the unused NRB can be transferred to their spouse or civil partner.
- The surviving spouse or civil partner will have the benefit of:
  - their own NRB, and
  - any unused percentage of their spouse's or civil partner's NRB
- The unused percentage is applied to the NRB at the time of the surviving spouse's or civil partner's death
  - **not** at the date of first death
- The executors of the surviving spouse or civil partner must claim the transferred NRB by the submission of the IHT return by the later of:
  - 2 years of the second death, or
  - 3 months of the executors starting to act

- As a result, each spouse or civil partner can now leave the whole of their estate to the surviving spouse or civil partner with no adverse IHT consequences.

Exam focus

Exam kit questions on this area:
- Surfe
- Pescara
- Kesme and Soba

Tax planning

Advice for couples:

- Where the couple own assets that qualify for BPR and/or APR these assets should **not** be left to the other spouse or civil partner.

   This is because the legacy would be covered by the inter-spouse exemption and the benefit of BPR and APR is lost.

- BPR and APR assets should be left to non exempt beneficiaries and other assets left to the spouse or civil partner.

   As a result, the benefit of both the relief and inter-spouse exemption will be available to reduce the value of the chargeable estate.

Inheritance tax

IHT and CGT on sales/gifts

Exam questions dealing with capital transactions may require consideration of both the IHT and CGT implications of transactions.

	CGT	IHT
Sale	Gain/loss in normal way	No IHT – no diminution in estate
Gift during lifetime	As for sale	CLT – tax now
	Gain/loss in normal way	PET – tax if die within 7 years
Gift on death	No CGT	Asset part of death estate
Possible reliefs		
– Business assets	Entrepreneurs' relief	APR/BPR
	Gift relief	**Note:** On a PET or CLT – reliefs only available if asset still owned by donee at date of donor's death
	Rollover relief	
	EIS/SEIS reinvestment relief	
– Non-business	PPR relief	None
	Gift relief if CLT for IHT purposes	
	EIS/SEIS reinvestment relief	

Advantage of lifetime gifts	Disadvantages of lifetime gifts

- Reduces IHT payable on death as assets gifted during lifetime are removed from the chargeable estate.
 	
  Note: no reduction in the value of the chargeable estate if the assets gifted get BPR or APR at 100%.
 	
- IHT on lifetime gifts likely to be less than IHT in death estate because:
  - IHT = Nil (for a PET) if the donor lives for > 7 years, and 20% (for CLT)
  - the value is frozen at the date of the gift, therefore by gifting an appreciating asset during lifetime, the IHT is based on a lower amount, and fall in value relief is available if fallen in value
  - the value subject to IHT is less as lifetime exemptions (such as AE, ME, small gift relief) available
  - taper relief available if the donor lives for > 3 years.
	- Loss of income and use of the capital if assets given away.
	- CGT may be payable if the assets gifted during lifetime are chargeable assets for CGT, whereas no CGT if gifted on death.
	- APR or BPR on lifetime gift withdrawn if donee does not retain asset at donor death. Therefore better to secure BPR/APR by retaining asset in donor's estate.

Exam focus

Exam kit questions on this area:
- Cada
- Stella and Maris
- Una

Skipping a generation

- Gifting to grandchildren rather then children avoids a further IHT charge when the children die
- Such planning requires children to be independently wealthy, such that they have no need for the inheritance.

chapter 9

Personal tax – overseas aspects

In this chapter

- Tax status.
- Domicile.
- Residence.
- Splitting the tax year.
- Income tax.
- Overseas employment income.
- Capital gains tax.
- Inheritance tax.

Personal tax – overseas aspects

Exam focus

The overseas aspects of income tax, capital gains tax and inheritance tax can feature as part of a question.

You must be able to deal with situations involving individuals either coming to or leaving the UK and with all of the taxes involved.

Tax status

- How an individual is assessed to income tax and capital gains tax depends on their:
  - Residency status, and,
  - Domicile.

Exam focus

You may be required to assess the residence or domicile position of an individual in a particular scenario. It is essential that you are familiar with these definitions.

Domicile

Definition

An individual's permanent home.

Domicile of origin:
- acquired at birth
- normally domicile of father.

Domicile of dependency
- up to the age of 16
- if father changes domicile, individual follows suit

Domicile of choice

(e.g. where an individual emigrates to another country)
- need to demonstrate severed all ties with UK.

Residence

Definition

An individual will be resident in the tax year if they:
- do not meet one of the **automatic non-UK residence tests**, and
- meet one of the **automatic UK residence tests**, or
- meet one or more of the **sufficient ties tests**.

Key Point

If an individual satisfies an automatic non-UK residence test and automatic UK residence test = non-UK resident.

Personal tax – overseas aspects

Resident in UK?

Automatic non-UK residency tests

Individual in UK in **tax year** less than
- **16 days,** or
- **46 days** and not UK R for last 3 years, or
- **91 days** and works FT abroad

Automatic UK residency tests

Individual in UK at least:
- **183 days** in tax year, or
- **30 days** in tax year and only home in UK, or
- **365 days** continuously, some in tax year and work FT

Sufficient ties tests

1. Close family resident in UK – Spouse/Civil partner/minor child
2. Accommodation in UK – available 91 consecutive days in tax year
3. Substantive work in UK – 40 days
4. Days in UK in last two tax years – > 90 days in either year
5. Country tie – Most time spent in UK

Previously resident = UK R in one of last 3 years

Consider **all five** ties

See tax tables in exam

Not previously resident = not UK R in any of last 3 years

Consider **first four** ties

Application of sufficient ties tests

Days spent in the UK	Previously resident	Not previously resident
Less than 16 days	Automatically **not** UK resident	Automatically **not** UK resident
16 to 45 days	Resident if: 4 UK ties (or more)	Automatically **not** UK resident
46 to 90 days	Resident if: 3 UK ties (or more)	Resident if: 4 UK ties
91 to 120 days	Resident if: 2 UK ties (or more)	Resident if: 3 UK ties (or more)
121 to 182 days	Resident if: 1 UK tie (or more)	Resident if: 2 UK ties (or more)
183 or more days	Automatically resident	Automatically resident

Note that this table will be provided in the tax rates and allowances.

Splitting tax year

Split year basis (SYB) can apply if individual = UK R in tax year under automatic tests or sufficent ties test.

- SYB = automatic if conditions satisfied
- Cannot disapply SYB

Key Point

- If non-UK R in the tax year
    - SYB cannot apply
    - Will be non-UK R for whole year

Personal tax – overseas aspects

SPLITTING TAX YEAR

Leaving the UK

Individual must be
- UK resident in current year, and
- UK resident in previous year, and
- not UK resident in the following year

Individual leaves the UK and:
1. Begins working full time abroad
2. Accompanies partner working full time abroad
3. Ceases to have any UK home

Overseas part starts:

Date start work abroad

Later of date
– Joins partner
– Partner starts work abroad
Date have no UK home

Arriving in the UK

Individual must be
- UK resident in current year, and
- Not UK resident in previous year

Individual arrives in the UK and:
1. Acquires a UK home
2. Begins working full time in the UK – For ≥ 365 days
3. Returns following a period when individual (or partner) worked full time overseas

UK part starts:

Date acquires UK home
Date start work in UK

Date individual (or partner) stops working overseas

Income tax

General rule:
- UK Resident
  - Taxed on UK and overseas income
- Non-resident
  - Taxed on UK income only
  - Personal allowance available against UK income for UK/EEA citizens

Key Point

- All income arising in the UK is always subject to UK income tax irrespective of individual's status.
- A UK resident is always taxed on overseas income
  - the only issue is whether they are taxed on an arising or remittance basis.

Personal tax – overseas aspects

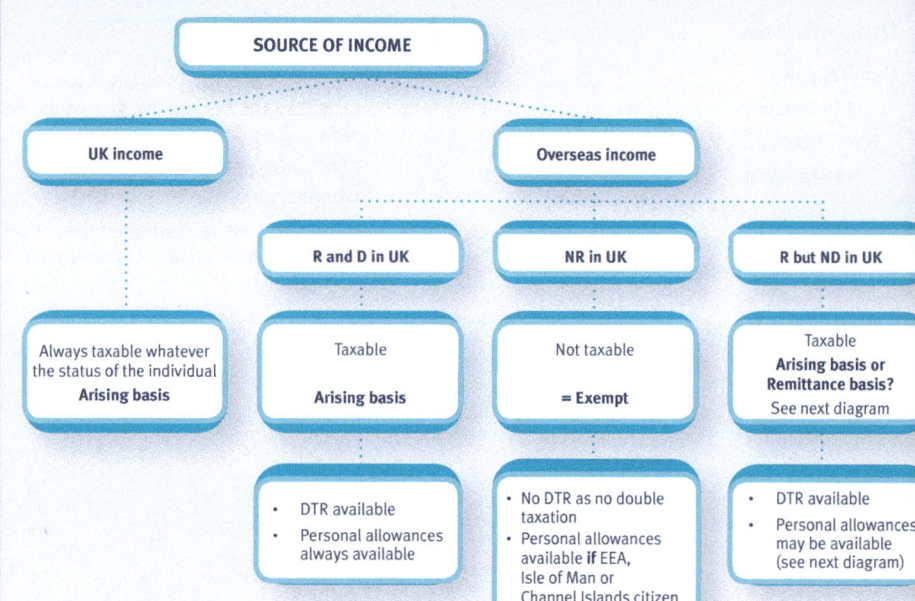

Chapter 9

```
                    R but ND in UK
                   /              \
            UK income          Overseas income
                |                   |
   Always taxable whatever    Taxable but depends on amount of
   the status of the individual   unremitted overseas income and gains
         Arising basis              /            \
                               ≤ £2,000        > £2,000
```

≤ £2,000:
- Remittance basis = automatic
- Personal allowance available

> £2,000:
- Arising basis = automatic
- Personal allowances available

But
- Can elect for Remittance basis (decision made each year)

If elect:
- Personal allowances not available
- Possible Remittance basis charge (RBC)

If taxed on a remittance basis:
- All overseas income = taxed as other income (including interest and dividends) (i.e. taxed at 20%/40%/45%)

DTR available

Definition of Remittance

Includes:

- Bringing overseas income directly into the UK except for amounts used to:
  - Invest in shares or make a loan to an unquoted trading company or member of a trading group
  - Pay the RBC.
- Using overseas income
  - to settle debts in the UK
  - to purchase goods and services which are subsequently brought into the UK

  Except:
  - personal items (e.g. clothes, jewellery)
  - items brought in for repair
  - items costing ≤ £1,000
  - items brought in temporarily.

Exam focus

Exam kit questions on this area:

- Shuttelle
- Piquet and Buraco
- Jodie

Remittance Basis Charge (RBC)

- Only levied if individual
  - aged ≥ 18 years old
  - is not UK Dom
  - is UK resident in current tax year
  - has been UK resident for 7 out of last 9 tax years
  - has total unremitted income and gains > £2,000, and
  - elects for the remittance basis to apply
- Additional tax charge:

	if UK resident for
£30,000 p.a.	7 out of last 9 tax years
£60,000 p.a.	12 out of last 14 tax years
£90,000 p.a.	17 out of last 20 tax years

- Added to income tax liability
- Paid under self-assessment

Exam focus

Exam kit questions on this area:

- Shuttelle

Personal tax – overseas aspects

Double tax relief

Deduct from the individual's income tax liability
Lower of:
- Overseas withholding tax suffered
- UK income tax on that source of overseas income

UK income tax attributable to a source of overseas income
= the reduction in the total income tax liability that would arise if that source of overseas income is excluded from taxable income.

To calculate UK income tax on overseas income:
- Always treat overseas income as the 'top slice' of income type
- Calculate total income tax **including** that source of overseas income
- Calculate total income tax **without** that source of overseas income
- Difference = UK income tax on that source income

If more than one source of overseas income:
- Need separate DTR calculation for each source of overseas income
- Take out the source with the **highest rate of overseas tax** first

Exam focus

You may be asked to consider the tax position of:

- an individual coming to work in the UK, or
- a UK individual leaving the UK to work abroad.

Exam kit questions on this area:

- Mirtoon

Overseas employment income

Basis of assessment:

- follows normal overseas income rules re-status of individual (see earlier diagram)
- but some exceptions

Earnings from duties performed in UK

- always taxable, regardless of tax status
- arising basis

Earnings from duties performed abroad

See diagram overleaf.

Personal tax – overseas aspects

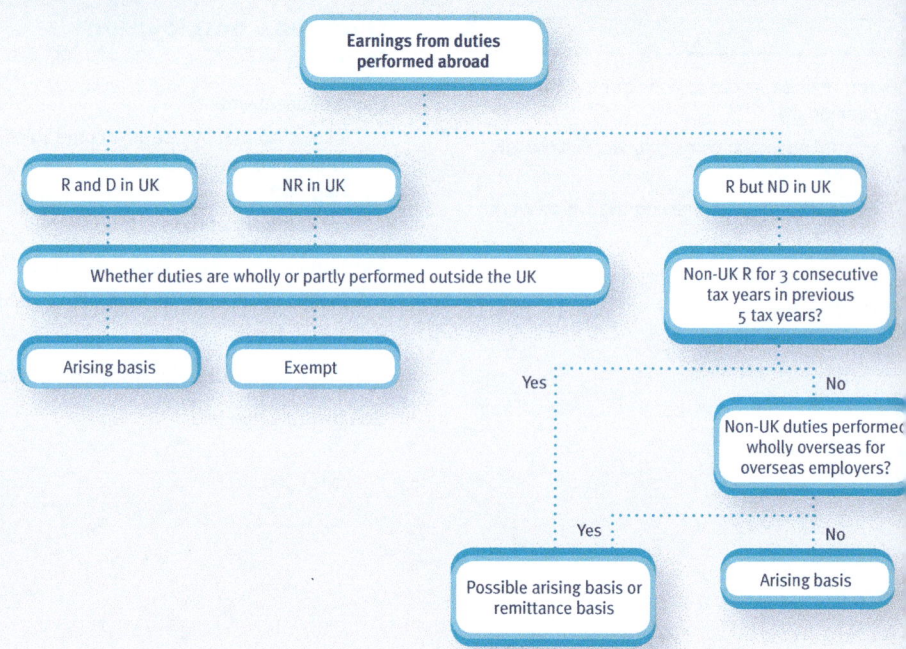

Chapter 9

UK individual leaving to work overseas

- If SYB applies, treated as
  - non UK resident
  - for whole of the period overseas.
- Travel and subsistence – allowable expenses:
  - travel to and from overseas employment at the beginning and end of contract
  - overseas board and lodgings in respect of overseas employment
  - unlimited return trips to the UK
  - family travel:
    - 2 visits/year
    - for spouse/children < 18 years old
    - provided employee overseas ≥ 60 continuous days
    - employer bears the cost.

Exam focus

Exam kit questions on this area:

- Jerome and Tricycle Ltd
- Spetz Ltd Group

Key Point

Individual comes to UK to take up employment

- Taxed under normal rules set out above.
- UK residency position depends on intentions when arrive in UK.
- Tax position resulting from residency position:
  - Taxed on all UK source income on an arising basis regardless of residency status
  - Overseas income:

    See earlier diagram.

Capital gains tax

- General rule:

Individual's status	Taxed on
R and domiciled in UK	Worldwide assets
Not R in UK, regardless of domicile	No liability on any assets (unless trading in UK, or UK residential property)
R in UK; but Not UK domiciled	UK gains – Arising basis Non UK gains – Possible remittance basis, see diagram

Personal tax – overseas aspects

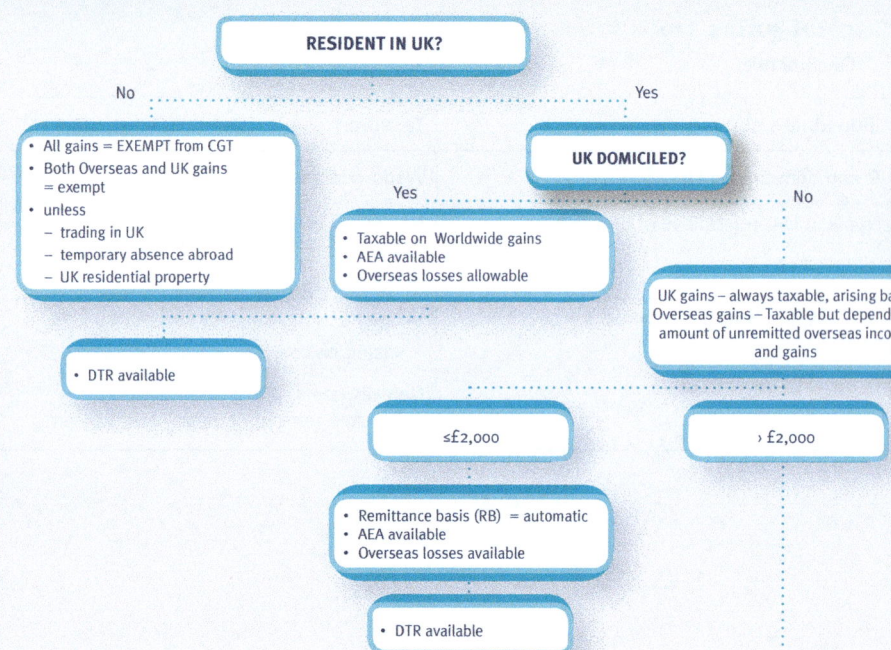

Chapter 9

- Arising basis = automatic
- AEA available
- Overseas losses allowable

BUT

- Can elect for RB (decision made each year)
- One election for both income tax and CGT

If elect:

- No AEA available
- Possible Remittance basis charge (RBC) of £30,000, £60,000 or £90,000?
  – see income tax section

If RB claimed – are overseas losses available?
= depends

DTR available

Make election
- Binding
- Irrevocable
- Overseas losses allowable
  – now and forever
- But subject to complicated matching rules (not examinable)

No election
- Overseas losses not allowable
  – now or ever

Individual coming to the UK

Key Point

Only taxed on gains made after becoming UK resident, subject to domicile rules for overseas assets.

Individual leaving the UK

Key Point

- If UK resident for 4 of the previous 7 tax years before leaving the UK
- UK residents remain liable to CGT even though no longer UK resident **if absent from UK for < 5 years**
- To avoid the rules and for gains to be exempt: (see diagram)

Exam focus

You may be asked to consider the CGT position of an individual coming to the UK and leaving the UK.

Exam focus

Exam kit questions on this area:

- Mirtoon
- Brad
- Jodie
- Cate and Ravi

Temporary absence abroad

```
            Individual leaving the UK for
             period of temporary absence
                        │
              Period whilst abroad:
                     No CGT
                        │
              On re-entry into the UK:
                   ┌────┴────┐
```

Return within five years:
Liable on
- disposals of all assets whilst abroad, if the asset was owned before leaving the UK
- disposals after the date of return

Return after five years:
Liable on
- disposals after the date of return only
- No CGT on disposals whilst abroad (unless UK residential property)

Non-UK residents and UK residential property disposals

The disposal of UK residential property by a non-UK resident individual:

- is a chargeable disposal, and
- a liability to CGT will arise, but
- only on gains accruing after 5 April 2015
- to the extent that they are not covered by
  - reliefs (e.g. PPR relief, rollover relief or gift relief), or
  - the AEA.

Methods of calculating the gain or loss

Property purchased after 5 April 2015:

- calculate gain (or loss) before reliefs in the normal way.

Property purchased before 5 April 2015:

- rebase the cost to market value at 5 April 2015 (automatic treatment without an election), or
- elect to time apportion gain pre and post 5 April 2015, or
- elect to be assessed on the whole gain or loss.

PPR relief for non-UK resident individuals

- Only consider period of ownership from April 2015 for PPR purposes (as only the gain arising after 5 April 2015 is taxable)
- PPR relief available as usual for periods of occupation and deemed occupation (see Chapter 6).
- For periods of non-occupation, if the individual/spouse/civil partner:
  - stayed in the property for at least 90 nights in the tax year
    = treat **whole tax year** as period of **occupation**
  - did not stay in the property for at least 90 nights in the tax year
    = treat the **whole tax year** as a period of **non-occupation**

Double tax relief

Double tax relief

Deduct from the individual's capital gains tax liability
Lower of:
- Overseas capital gains tax suffered
- UK capital gains tax on the disposal of that overseas asset

Note:

- The AEA amount is allocated against UK gains first.
- When calculating UK tax on overseas gains, treat as 'top slice'

Inheritance tax

- General rule:

Individual's status	Taxed on
UK domiciled	Worldwide assets
Not UK domiciled	UK assets only

- Deemed domicile
    - An individual who ceases to be UK domiciled remains deemed UK domiciled for IHT purposes for a further 3 years.
    - An individual who has been resident in the UK for ≥ 17 out of the previous 20 tax years is deemed UK domiciled.

Key Point

Liability to IHT is determined by domicile, not residency.

Location of assets
(only relevant to non-UK domiciled individuals)

Land and buildings	• Physical location
Registered shares and securities	• Place of registration
Chattels	• Location at time of transfer
Debtors	• Where the debtor resides
Bank accounts	• Location of account
Life assurance policies	• Where proceeds are payable
Interest in a business	• Where the business is carried on

Exam focus

You may be asked to consider the IHT position of an individual coming to the UK and leaving the UK.

Individual leaving the UK

Key Point

- Liable to IHT on worldwide assets
  - for 3 years after leaving UK (deemed UK domiciled).
- If acquire a non UK domicile of choice:
  - will only be liable on UK assets once 3 years have elapsed.

Individual coming to the UK

Key Point

- If acquire a UK domicile of choice:
  - liable on worldwide assets when become UK domiciled.
- If remain non UK domiciled:
  - deemed UK domiciled and liable on worldwide assets when been resident in UK for 17 out of last 20 tax years.

Exam focus

Exam kit questions on this area:

- Ash
- Kesme and Soba

Double tax relief

Deduct:

- from IHT on estate
- after QSR
- Lower of:
  - overseas death duties
  - UK IHT on overseas asset.

Note:

- UK IHT on overseas asset
  = (Amount included in estate)
  × average rate of IHT after QSR.

Personal tax – overseas aspects

chapter 10

Trusts

In this chapter

- Overview of trusts.
- Types of trust.
- Financial planning benefits of trusts.
- Income tax.
- Capital taxes and trusts.

Overview of trusts

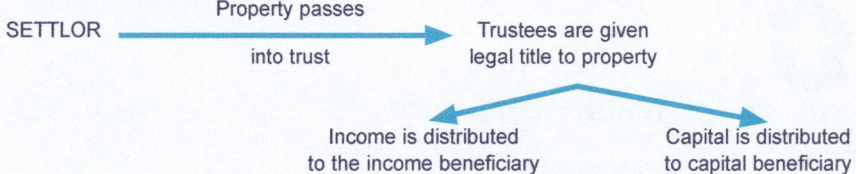

- Trust (also known as a settlement) = Treated as separate taxable person.
- Must have > one trustee.
- Trustees = act in representative capacity in best interests of beneficiaries.
- Trust deed = details trustee's powers and duties.

Exam focus

The rules for the taxation of trusts changed with effect from 22 March 2006, but knowledge of pre 22 March 2006 trusts is not examinable.

In recognition of the complexity of trusts, the examining team has confirmed that the knowledge required in relation to trusts is summarised in this chapter.

Types of trust

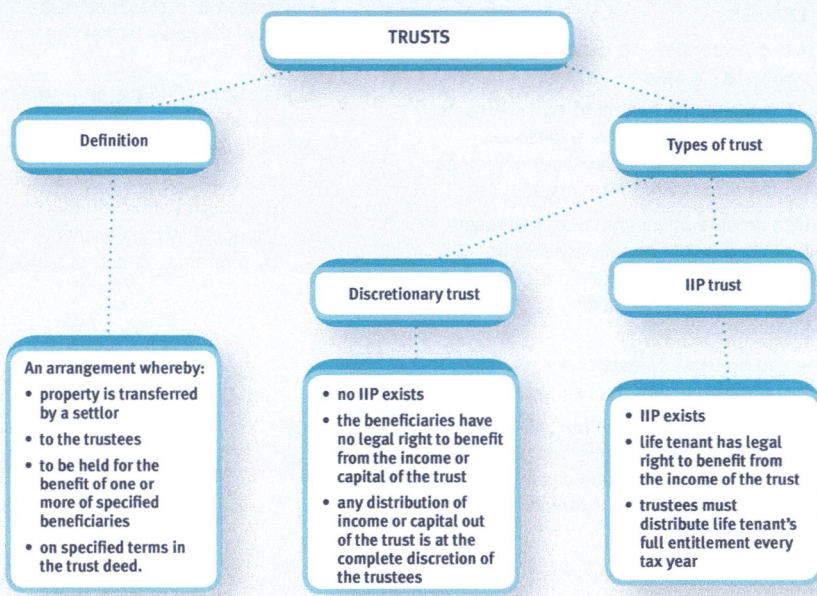

Financial planning benefits of trusts

- A trust separates the beneficial and legal ownership of assets:
  - enables the benefit of owning assets (e.g. income), to be enjoyed by someone (the beneficiary) other than the legal owner (the trustees).
- Can provide an income from the assets for one group of beneficiaries while preserving and protecting the capital for others, for example, setting up an IIP trust:
  - to protect interests of children in situation where spouse remarries
  - to transfer assets under will to IIP trust with spouse (life tenant) entitled to income for life and capital assets passing to children (remaindermen) on spouse's death.
- Can provide a means for an older generation to protect and make financial provision for next generation or grandchildren.
- Can provide a flexible arrangement where different beneficiaries have different needs.
  - For example, a settlor creates a DT whereby trustees have discretion to distribute income/assets to children by reference to individual need.

Income tax

- Trustees = separate taxable person.
- Income tax paid by trustees under self-assessment on income generated by trust and by beneficiaries on income received.

Type	Trustees	Beneficiaries
IIP	Depends on type of income: • dividends 10% • savings 20% • other 20%	• Annuitant entitled to fixed amount of income each year (annuity). • Life tenant entitled to the remaining trust income. • Taxed on his entitlement – even if not distributed. • Income maintains nature in beneficiaries' hands (i.e. savings income and other income grossed up by 100/80 with a 20% tax credit, divided income grossed up by 100/90 with 10% tax credit).
DT	Different rates – calculation not examinable	• Taxed on income actually received in tax year. • Always grossed up at 100/55 with 45% tax credit.

Capital taxes and trusts

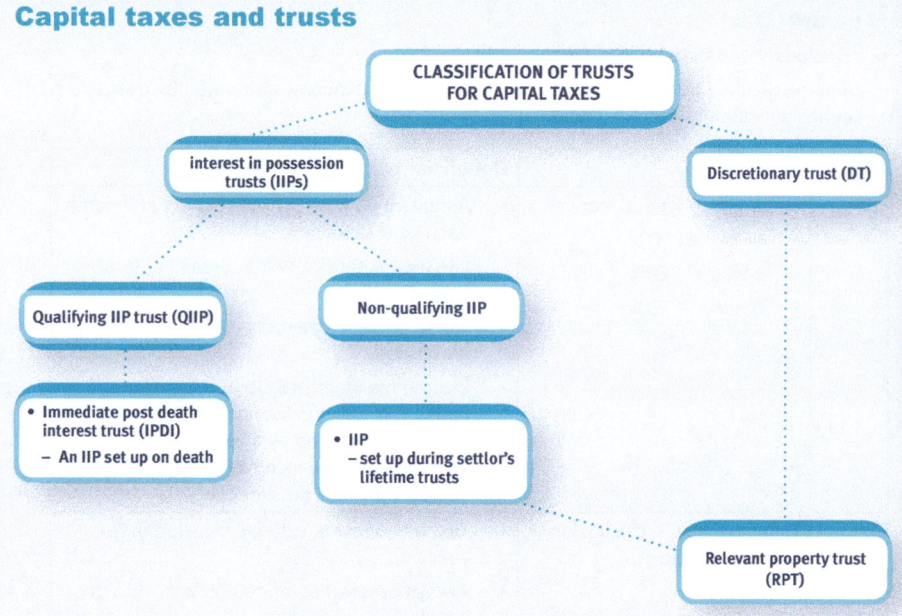

Chapter 10

Inheritance tax

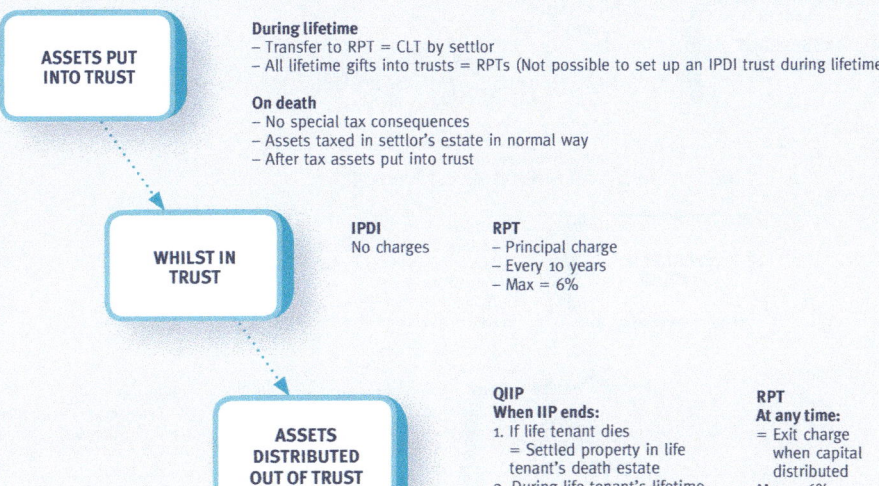

Trusts

Capital Gains Tax

ASSETS PUT INTO TRUST

For all trusts
During lifetime
- Chargeable disposal of asset
- Calculate gain using MV as consideration
- Gift relief available on ANY asset as there is an immediate charge to IHT
- Trustees base cost = MV less gift relief

On death
- No CGT consequences on death
- Not a chargeable disposal
- Trusts acquire assets at probate value

WHILST IN TRUST

All trusts
- Chargeable gains on disposals by trustees
- AEA = half individual's AEA (£5,550 in 2015/16)
- Rate of tax = 28%
- Trustees pay out of trust fund
- Assessed under self-assessment rules

ASSETS DISTRIBUTED OUT OF TRUST

IPDI ends
– interest ends on death of life tenant
= No CGT
= Tax free uplift to MV
Remainderman receives assets at MV on life tenant's death

Any trust
– in any other circumstances
= Chargeable disposal
- Gift relief on ANY assets as IHT charge
- unless IPDI
= qualifying assets only

Tax planning opportunities

- Gifting assets into a trust during lifetime
  - means that assets not in settlor's estate on death.
- Assets which appreciate in value can be transferred into the trust
  - will increase in value outside of both the settlor's and the beneficiaries estates.
- Exit charges and principal charges = max 6%
  - may not be significant in the context of the financial planning requirements.
- Trustees of a DT can choose to give income to non-tax paying beneficiaries
  - repayment of income tax paid by the trustees can be claimed.

Exam focus

Exam kit questions on this area:
- Farina and Lauda
- King
- Surfe

Trusts

chapter 11

Ethics, personal financial management and self-assessment

In this chapter

- Professional Code of Ethics.
- Monitoring of serious tax offenders.
- Personal financial management.
- Key investment products.
- Tax efficient investment schemes.
- Sources of finance.
- Self-assessment.

Ethics, personal financial management and self-assessment

Exam focus

This chapter covers the very important topics of ethics, professional issues, personal financial management and self-assessment.

The examining team has stated that there will always be up to 5 marks in section A of each exam allocated to the topic of ethics and professional issues.

Questions will require you to provide practical advice based on a particular set of facts.

You need a good knowledge of the professional code of ethics and the investment products available.

You must be able to give suitable advice based on the facts of a particular scenario.

Professional Code of Ethics

Principles

- **O**bjectivity.
- **P**rofessional behavour.
- **P**rofessional competence.
- **I**ntegrity.
- **C**onfidentiality.

Key Point

Remember: OPPIC.

Exam focus

Exam kit questions on this area:

- Drench, Hail Ltd and Rain Ltd
- Jonny

Chapter 11

New clients

Before taking a new client – a member of ACCA must assess:

- risk to the integrity of the practice on accepting work
- whether firm has adequate skills and competence
- risk of money laundering.

Information to be obtained:

- For a company
  - proof of incorporation, primary business address and registered office
  - structure, directors and shareholders of the company
  - identities of persons instructing the firm on behalf of the company and persons authorised to do so.

- For an individual
  - proof of identity and residential address
  - details of nature and structure of any unincorporated business interests and persons authorised to act on behalf of the business (e.g. partners in a partnership).

On accepting work – a member of ACCA

- must ask permission from the client to contact old advisers to request information
- if client refuses, should consider not acting for them
- if not, issue a letter of engagement setting out terms and conditions.

Exam focus

Exam kit questions on this area:

- Farina and Lauda

Ethics, personal financial management and self-assessment

Conflicts of interest

- Examples:
  - asked to act for another party in a transaction with an existing client
  - acting for both parties in a divorce
  - acting for the employer and their employees
  - where the adviser may benefit from the transaction.
- A member of ACCA may act for both parties if safeguards put in place:
  - the potential conflict should be pointed out to all relevant parties
  - consent should be obtained to act for them
  - the firm must have clear guidelines in relation to confidentiality, and
  - should consider the need to use separate teams for each client.
- Alternatively, consider acting for just one party, or not acting for either party.

Exam focus

Exam kit questions on this area:

- Farina and Lauda

Dealing with HMRC

- Information provided must be accurate and complete.
- Must not assist a client to plan or commit an offence.
- If become aware of a tax irregularity
  - discuss with client
  - ensure proper disclosure to HMRC.
- Client error
  - decide whether genuine or deliberate/fraudulent act
  - explain to client the need to notify HMRC
  - prompt/adequate disclosure taken into account when deciding penalties
  - if client refuses
    - must explain potential consequences in writing
    - if material, consider whether to continue to act for client
  - if client still refuses
    - should cease to act and write to HMRC stating that the firm no longer acts for the client but not stating the reason why.

Exam focus

Exam kit questions on this area:

- Flame plc Group
- Ziti
- Kantar

Money laundering regulations

Definition

Money laundering = benefiting from or concealing the proceeds of crime

- includes the proceeds of tax evasion.

A member of ACCA must appoint a Money laundering reporting officer (MLRO):

- decides whether to report a transaction to the National Crime Agency (NCA)
- if a report is made, client should not be informed as this is an offence (known as 'tipping off').

Employees

If a member is an employee and becomes aware of irregularities in their firm's dealings with HMRC:

- raise concerns with the appropriate person
- if appropriate action not taken
  - seek advice from ACCA
- in addition, consider:
  - need to report to MLRO
  - resigning from employment
  - need to disclose under the Public Interest Disclosure Act.

Chapter 11

Tax evasion versus tax avoidance

- Tax evasion
  - unlawful
  - e.g. suppressing information or submitting false information
  - client = subject to criminal prosecution / fines / imprisonment
  - adviser = subject to sanctions of criminal law.
- Tax avoidance
  - use of the taxation system to legitimately reduce tax
  - e.g. advice to reduce tax liability.
  - also used to describe tax schemes devised to utilise loopholes in the tax legislation.
- Specific schemes have been targeted with anti-avoidance legislation.

- HMRC have also introduced:
  - Disclosure obligations re specific tax avoidance schemes.

A general anti-abuse rule (GAAR) to counter artificial and abusive schemes to avoid tax.

This targets arrangements which cannot be regarded as a reasonable course of action.

Exam focus

Exam kit questions on this area:

- Una
- Opus Ltd Group

Monitoring of serious tax offenders

Those who:

- incur a penalty for deliberate evasion
- in respect of tax of £5,000 or more

will be required to submit returns:

- for up to the following 5 years
- showing more detailed business accounts information, and
- detailing the nature and value of any balancing adjustments within the accounts.

Dishonest conduct of tax agents

- Incurs a civil penalty of up to £50,000
- In cases where full disclosure was not made, HMRC may:
  - publish details of the penalised tax agent.
  - access the working papers of a dishonest agent with agreement of the Tax tribunal.

Publication of names of tax offenders

- HMRC have the power to publish:
  - the names and details
  - of individuals and companies
  - who are penalised for deliberate defaults leading to a loss of tax of > £25,000.
- Names will not be published of:
  - those who make a full unprompted disclosure, or
  - a full prompted disclosure within the required time.

Giving advice to clients

Considerations of accountants	Factors relating to client to consider
• Know the Professional Code of Ethics.	• Personal objectives.
• Know your client – fact find.	• Current position.
• Best advice – advice must be suitable.	• Dependants.
• Best execution – obtain best price.	• Age.
• Switching – avoid unnecessary transactions.	• Risk acceptable.
• Key features – explain why course of action recommended.	• Tax status.
	• Tax efficiency.
	• Liquidity.

Personal financial management

Individuals must balance the need for income on an on-going basis with investing for capital growth to be used to fund retirement.

Suitable investments will change during an individual's lifetime as lifestyle and income streams change.

Factors to consider when making investments:

- Income available after meeting current obligations.
- Desire to own home and method of financing.
- Need to fund children's education.
- Responsibility to support parents.
- Required lifestyle on retirement.
- Desire to leave an inheritance to children.
- Need to ensure some investments are readily realisable to fund immediate unforeseen demands.
- Likelihood of receiving an inheritance.
- Attitude to risk.

Key investment products

Consider features of different investments to determine if they meet the needs of the client.

	IT free	CGT free	Risk	Liquidity	Income/ capital growth
Bank/ B Soc a/cs	x	N/A	L	L_1	I
NS&I					
– Direct Saver a/c	x	N/A	RF	L_1	I
– Investment a/c	x	N/A	RF	L_1	I
NS&I savings certificates	3	3	RF	L_2	I
Premium bonds	3	3	RF	L_1	–
Children's bonus bonds	3	3	L	L_2	C
Qualifying life assurance policies	3	3	L	L_3	C
EIS and SEIS scheme	Tax relief on investment but income taxable	3	VH	L_3	C
VCT scheme	Tax relief on investment and dividends tax free	3	H	L_1	C

Chapter 11

	IT free	CGT free	Risk	Liquidity	Income/ capital growth
Pension schemes (Tax relief on payments)	3	3	M	L_3	C
QCBs	x	3	M	L_1	C/I
Gilts	x	3	L	L_1	I
Land and buildings	x	x	M	L_3	C/I
REITs, Investment trusts, unit trusts and open ended investment companies	x	x	M	L_1	C
Quoted shares/securities	x	x	M/H	L_1	C
Unquoted shares/securities	x	x	VH	L_3	C/I
Individual savings accounts	3	3	L/M	L_1	C/I

Key

I	Income	H	High risk
C	Capital growth	VH	Very high risk
x	Chargeable	L_1	Immediate access
3	Tax-free	L_2	Access possible but penalty
L	Low risk	L_3	Non liquid
M	Medium risk	RF	Risk-free
		N/A	Not applicable

Tax efficient investment schemes

Special tax relief to encourage investment by individuals in riskier small companies.

	EIS	SEIS	VCT
Qualifying Individual	• Subscribes in cash • New ordinary shares • Qualifying company • Own $\leq$ 30% of ordinary share capital		• Subscribes • Newly issued shares
	• Not employee or director • Independent of company prior to first issue	• Not current employee (can be director or previous employee)	
Qualifying company/VCT	• Unquoted trading company • Have a permanent establishment in UK		• VCT must be quoted on a stock exchange in EEA • Qualifying investment = in EIS qualifying companies • Approved by HMRC
	• Full time employees $\leq$ 250 • Gross assets $\leq$ £15m before and $\leq$ £16m after subscription	• Full time employees < 25 • Gross assets $\leq$ £200,000 before subscription • Not previously have used EIS or VCT • Carrying on trade < 2 years old, or preparing to carry on trade	

	EIS	SEIS	VCT
Maximum funds company can raise	• £5 million in any 12 months • 12 million lifetime total	• £150,000 in any 3 years	• £5 million in any 12 months • 12 million lifetime total
Investment by individual	• Max £1 million p.a.	• Max £100,000 p.a.	• Max £200,000 p.a.
Retention period for IT relief	• 3 years • IT relief withdrawn if sold within 3 years		• 5 years • IT relief withdrawn if sold within 5 years
IT relief: Deduct from IT liability	• % of amount subscribed: = 30%	• % of amount subscribed: = 50%	• % of amount subscribed: = 30%
Carryback amount to previous year	• Any amount invested, but cannot get relief on more than £1 million in any one tax year	• Any amount invested, but cannot get relief on more than £100,000 in any one tax year	• No carryback
CGT on disposal	• Gain – Exempt if held > 3 yrs • Loss – Allowable – can convert into IT loss		• No gain or loss whenever sold

	EIS	SEIS	VCT
Reinvestment relief (chapter 6)	• Gain on any chargeable asset = deferred to subject to conditions • Gain crystallises when EIS shares disposed of or investor/spouse/civil partner emigrates < 3 years	• Up to a maximum of 50% of gain on any chargeable asset = exempt subject to conditions • Relief withdrawn if SEIS shares sold < 3 years	• No relief
IHT – BPR	• 100% if owned ≥ 2 yrs		• No BPR
Dividends	• Taxable		• Tax free on investment within annual limit

Exam focus

Exam kit questions on this area:

- Tetra
- Pescara

Sources of finance

Personal

Mortgage
- lowest interest rate (cheap)
- longest term – secured on house.

Secured loan
- cheap, can be long term.

Unsecured loan
- more expensive
- normally < 5 yrs.

Hire purchase
- more expensive
- normally 1 – 5 yrs.

Overdraft
- expensive, short term, repayable on demand.

Credit cards
- most expensive (except zero per cent cards).

Business

Equity
- does not need to be repaid
- dividends can vary each year, not tax deductible
- outside influence
- e.g. share issue, EIS and VCT schemes.

Debt
- must be repaid
- interest payments fixed, but tax deductible.

Long term debt
- for purchase of assets, provision of working capital
- e.g. term loan, mortgage, debenture.

Short term debt
- e.g. overdraft, trade credit, debt factoring.

Self-assessment

Filing for 2015/16 returns

- Later of:
    - 31 October 2016 (paper return).
    - 31 January 2017 (electronic return).
    - Three months after issue of the notice to file a return.
- Fixed and tax geared penalties may apply for late filing (see later).

Notification of chargeability

- Must notify HMRC of income or chargeable gains on which tax is due
    - Within 6 months of end of tax year in which the liability arises
    - i.e. by 5 October 2016 for 2015/16
- Standard penalty may apply for failure to notify of chargeability (see later).

Amendments to the return

- HMRC can amend return < 9 months of the actual filing date.
- Taxpayer can amend < 12 months of the 31 January filing date.

Determination of tax

- Issued by HMRC when a return is not filed by the 31 January filing date.
- Can be issued by HMRC within 3 years from the filing date (i.e. by 31 January 2020 for 2015/16 tax return).
- Assessment = replaced by the actual self-assessment return when it is submitted.

Records

Business records

- A business must keep records of:
  - all receipts and expenses
  - all goods purchased and sold
  - all supporting documents relating to the transactions of the business, such as accounts, books, contracts, vouchers and receipts.
- Self-employed taxpayers must retain all their records (not just business records) for five years after the 31 January filing date.
  For 2015/16 = until 31 January 2022.

Other records

- Other taxpayers should keep evidence of income received.
- Must normally be retained for 12 months after the 31 January filing date.
  For 2015/16 = until 31 January 2018

Penalty

- A fixed penalty of up to £3,000 may be charged for failure to keep or retain adequate records.

Payment dates for 2015/16

Payments on account (POAs)

- 31 January 2016.
- 31 July 2016.

Balancing payment

- 31 January 2017.

POAs = half previous years' tax payable by self-assessment and class 4 NIC (relevant amount)

- No POA if:
  - relevant amount for previous year is ≤ £1,000, or
  - more than 80% of the income tax liability of the previous year was collected at source.

Late payment interest

Charged on:
- all late payments of tax
- at a daily rate
- runs from: due date
- to: date of payment

Repayment interest

HMRC pay interest on overpaid tax
- from: later of
  - date tax due, or
  - date HMRC received tax
- to: date of repayment

Exam focus

Exam kit questions on this area:
- Una
- Ash
- Kantar

Standard penalties

Applies in two circumstances:

- Submission of incorrect returns
  - All taxes
- Failure to notify liability to tax
  - Income tax, CGT, Corporation tax, VAT and NIC
- Penalty = % of potential lost revenue
- Depends on the behaviour of the taxpayer

Taxpayer behaviour	Maximum penalty (% of revenue lost)
Genuine mistake (for incorrect returns only)	No penalty
Careless / Failure to take reasonable care	30%
Deliberate but no concealment	70%
Deliberate with concealment	100%

- Penalties may be reduced at HMRC discretion, where the taxpayer informs HMRC
  - larger reductions for unprompted disclosure

- Minimum penalties apply and vary based on:
  - the taxpayer's behaviour, and
  - whether disclosure is prompted or unprompted.
- An unprompted disclosure
  = where the taxpayer informs HMRC when they have no reason to believe HMRC have or are about to discover the error.
- Taxpayer can appeal against a standard penalty.

Exam focus

Exam kit questions on this area:

- Una
- Cuthbert

Other penalties relating to individuals

Offence	Penalty
Late filing of self-assessment tax return	
– filed after due date	£100 fixed penalty
Additional penalties:	
– filed 3 months late	Daily penalties of £10 per day (maximum of 90 days) in addition to £100 fixed penalty
– filed 6 months late	5% of tax due (minimum £300) plus above penalties
– more than 12 months after filing date where withholding information was:	The penalties above plus:
– not deliberate	Additional 5% of tax due (minimum £300)
– deliberate but no concealment	70% of tax due (minimum £300)
– deliberate with concealment	100% of tax due (minimum £300)

Chapter 11

Offence	Penalty
Late payment of tax • Paid > 1 month late • Paid > 6 months late • Paid > 12 months late	 5% of tax due Additional 5% Additional 5% Applies to balancing payment only (not POAs)

Fraud or negligence on claiming reduced POAs	£
	POAs if claim not made X
	Less: POAs actually paid (X)
	        ___
	        X

Failure to keep and retain required records	Up to £3,000 per year of assessment

Note that 'tax' for an individual will include income tax, capital gains tax and NIC.

Ethics, personal financial management and self-assessment

HMRC compliance checks

- HMRC has the right to enquire into the completeness and accuracy of any return
- Must issue written notice before commencing a compliance check (enquiry)
  - within 12 months of the date the return is actually filed
- On completion of a compliance check, HMRC must send the taxpayer a completion notice:
  - either stating no amendment required, or
  - amending the taxpayer's self-assessment
- Taxpayer has 30 days to appeal against HMRC's amendment.

Discovery assessments

- HMRC can raise a discovery assessment if they discover an inaccuracy in the return within

	Time from end of tax year	For 2015/16
Basic time limit	4 years	5 April 2020
Careless error	6 years	5 April 2022
Deliberate error	20 years	5 April 2036

Information and inspection powers

- Covers income tax, capital gains tax, corporation tax, VAT and PAYE.
- HMRC can request information from taxpayers
  - by a written information notice.
- Requests to third parties for information must normally
  - be agreed by the taxpayer, or
  - approved by the first-tier tribunal
- HMRC also has new powers to
  - enter and inspect a taxpayer's business premises
  - in order to inspect business records and assets.

Appeals to resolve disputes with HMRC

- Taxpayer can appeal against a decision made by HMRC
  - in writing
  - within 30 days of the disputed decision.
- They can proceed in one of two ways:
  - request a review by another HMRC officer, or
  - refer case to an independent Tax Tribunal.

Tax Tribunals

Two tiers (layers) of Tax Tribunal system:

- First-tier Tribunal, and
- Upper Tribunal.

The First-tier Tribunal deals with:

- Default paper cases:
  - simple appeals (e.g. against a fixed penalty)
  - usually no hearing provided both sides agree.
- Basic cases:
  - straightforward appeals
  - minimal exchange of paperwork
  - a short hearing.
- Standard cases:
  - more detailed consideration of issues
  - more formal hearing.
- Complex cases:
  - may be heard by the First Tier
  - however usually heard by Upper Tribunal.

The Upper Tribunal will deal with:

- Complex cases
  - requiring detailed specialist knowledge
  - a formal hearing.

Hearings are held in public and decisions are published.

A decision of the Upper Tribunal:

- may be appealed to the Court of Appeal
- but only on grounds of a point of law.

chapter 12

Personal tax planning

In this chapter

- Personal tax planning – overview.
- Income tax planning.
- Capital gains tax planning.
- Inheritance tax planning.
- Tax efficient income.
- Tax efficient expenditure.
- Tax efficient remuneration.
- Employment versus self-employment.
- Married couples/civil partners tax planning.
- Lifetime giving versus legacies on death.

Personal tax planning

Exam focus

In the exam you may need to be able to identify and advise on the types of investment and other expenditure that will result in a reduction in income tax liabilities for an individual.

You must also be able to identify the appropriate taxes applicable to a given scenario and advise on suitable tax planning measures to mitigate the personal tax liabilities of an individual.

Personal tax planning – overview

Personal tax planning involves consideration of the

- income tax
- NIC
- capital gains tax
- inheritance tax, and
- stamp taxes

implications of various courses of action.

Primary aim = usually to maximise the individual's 'net after tax cash flow' position.

Income tax planning

Standard income tax planning measures include:

- investing in tax efficient income
- incurring tax efficient expenditure
- maximising use of allowances and basic rate band
- negotiating tax efficient remuneration
- tax planning for married couples/civil partners.

Capital gains tax planning

Standard capital gains tax planning measures include:

- maximising use of AEA
- paying tax at lowest rate
- effective utilisation of capital losses
- effective use of CGT reliefs
- timing the acquisition and disposal of capital assets
- tax planning for married couples/civil partners.

Inheritance tax planning

Standard inheritance tax planning measures include:

- maximising use of lifetime exemptions (e.g. annual exemption, marriage exemption, small gifts, normal expenditure out of income)
- making lifetime gifts of appreciating assets (but be aware of CGT implications)
- making PETs as soon as possible (exempt if survive seven years)
- effective use of IHT reliefs
- maximising use of the nil rate band
- use of a deed of variation.

Common exam scenarios:

- Recommending tax efficient income and expenditure.
- Considering alternative forms of remuneration.
  - Employment versus self-employment.
- Tax planning for married couples/civil partners.
- Lifetime giving versus leaving a legacy in a will.

Tax efficient income
- Exempt income – Chapter 1.
- Tax exempt benefits – Chapter 2.

Tax efficient expenditure

	Maximum rate of tax relief
• Pension contributions	45%
• Qualifying loan interest	45% on up to greater of £50,000 or 25% of ATI
• Employment expenses	45%
• EIS investment	30% on investment up to £1 million
• SEIS investment	50% on investment up to £100,000
• VCT investment	30% on investment up to £200,000

Personal tax planning

Tax efficient remuneration

- Maximising use of exempt benefits
  - Chapter 2.
- Considering the provision of company car versus self purchase and mileage allowance or cash alternative (below).
- Receiving approved versus unapproved share options – Chapter 2.
- Comparing employment packages
  - Chapter 2.

Exam focus

Exam kit questions on this area:

- Jerome and Tricycle Ltd
- Hyssop Ltd

Company car versus self purchase and mileage allowance or cash alternative

Company car	Self purchase and mileage allowance or cash alternative

• Additional income tax liability on
   – Assessable car benefit
   – Possible fuel benefit.
• No running costs borne by individual employee.
• Employer liable to class 1A NICs.
• Costs of providing car and fuel, including class 1A NICs
  = allowable deductions against trading profits.
	• If mileage allowance received > AMAP: additional income tax liability and class 1 NICs payable on excess.
	• If mileage allowance received < AMAP: allowable deduction from employment income.
	• Additional income tax and class 1 NICs liability on any cash alternative received.
	• Individual employee bears running costs of car.
	• Employer liable to class 1 secondary NICs on excess mileage allowance and cash alternative.
	• Mileage allowance, or cash alternative, including class 1 NICs
	  = allowable deductions against trading profits.

Employment versus self-employment

- Decision = based on facts.
- No one factor is overriding.
- Consider all of the facts presented and apply the following factors:

Factors to consider	Employed Contract of service	Self-employed Contract for services
Control of work	Employee is directed/instructed in how and when to work by the employer.	Can choose hours, method, location and can sub-contract work to others. Is contracted to produce a result and is not directed in how to achieve that result.
Obligations	Employee has right to expect work and can not decline the work nor sub-contract the work to others outside the organisation.	Has no right to expect further work once the contract is completed and has no obligation to perform further work.
Risk	No personal financial risk to own capital, not responsible for correction of bad work, paid regardless of whether or not the business is profitable.	Risk financial loss of capital, personally responsible for correction of bad work, risk of no return if loss-making.

Factors to consider	Employed Contract of service	Self-employed Contract for services
Pay	Governed by employment legislation (i.e. regular pay, holiday pay, sick pay) and paid under PAYE system.	No employment rights, paid when work completed and invoice rendered.
Equipment	Employer provides.	Provides own.
Clients	Usually works wholly or mainly for one organisation.	Usually works for many customers.

Personal tax planning

- Employed = assessed according to employment income rules
  - On a receipts basis.
  - Allowable deductions = wholly, exclusively and necessarily incurred.
  - class 1 NICs payable.
  - Tax collected under PAYE.
- Self-employed = assessed according to trading income rules
  - On a current year basis.
  - Allowable deductions = wholly and exclusively incurred.
  - class 2 and 4 NICs payable.
  - Tax collected under self-assessment.
- Advantages of self-employment
  - More allowable expense deductions.
  - Lower total NICs payable.
  - Later payment of income tax and NICs.

Married couples/civil partners tax planning

Income tax

The following income tax planning advice should be given to married couples and couples in a civil partnership:

- Equalise income.
- Maximise use of tax free investments.
- Maximise pension contributions.
- Maximise use of available allowances.

Exam focus

Exam kit questions on this area:

- Monisha and Horner

- Equalising income
- Aim = to ensure full use of the couple's PAs and BRBs, and to minimise that amount of tax liable at the higher rate/additional rate.
- Consider ownership of income producing assets (i.e. sole versus joint ownership).
- Make declaration to vary the split of joint income if advantageous.
- Redistribute income producing assets to minimise the couple's liability.

Spouse as partner or employee

- Employment income is not transferable but if one of the couple is a sole trader, consider implications of creating a partnership with the spouse versus employing the spouse.

Partner	Employee
- split income in any proportion, as desired	- income tax relief on gross employment costs
- no tax relief for drawings	- class 1 primary and secondary contributions payable
- class 2 and 4 NICs payable	

Capital gains tax

The ability to transfer capital assets between spouses/civil partners with no CGT consequences provides the opportunity to:

- Effectively equalise income (as above) without incurring CGT.
- Ensure both spouses/civil partners use their AEAs each year.
- Ensure gains are realised by the spouse/civil partner who has capital losses.
- Ensure remaining gains are left with the spouse with the lowest income.

Chapter 12

Inheritance tax

- skip a generation
  (i.e. gift to grandchildren)
  - no immediate IHT saving
  - IHT saved on death of children
- enter into deed of variation to increase legacies to:
  - spouse/civil partner, and/or
  - charity to reduce the rate of tax
- if recipient spouse/civil partner is non-UK domiciled
  - consider election to be treated as UK domiciled

Exam focus

Exam kit questions on IHT planning:

- Brad

Lifetime giving versus legacies on death

Advantage of lifetime gifts	Disadvantages of lifetime gifts

• Reduces IHT payable on death as assets gifted during lifetime are removed from the chargeable estate.
 	
  Note – no reduction in the value of the chargeable estate if the assets gifted get BPR or APR at 100%.
 	
• IHT on lifetime gifts likely to be less than IHT in death estate because:
  – IHT = Nil if the donor lives for > 7 years.
  – the value is frozen at the date of the gift, therefore by gifting an appreciating asset during lifetime, the IHT is based on a lower amount.
  – the value subject to IHT is less as lifetime exemptions such AE, ME, small gift relief available.
  – taper relief available if the donor lives for > 3 years.
	• Loss of income and use of the capital if assets given away.
	
	• CGT may be payable if the assets gifted during lifetime are chargeable assets for CGT whereas no CGT if gifted on death.
	
	• APR or BPR on lifetime gift withdrawn if donee does not retain asset at donor death, better to secure BPR/APR by retaining asset in donor's estate.

chapter 13

Business tax

In this chapter

- Starting in business.
- Cash basis for small businesses.
- Flat rate expense deduction.
- Cessation of business.
- Trading losses.
- Partnerships.
- Self-assessment for the self-employed.

Business tax

Exam focus

For unincorporated businesses (which includes sole traders and partnerships) there is little new technical knowledge at P6 but you must now be able to handle business tax within a multi-tax scenario.

Be prepared to evaluate alternative strategies (e.g. in relation to losses), and to explain your recommendations.

Decision making is also likely to be a key area including 'lease versus buy' decisions and whether it is better from a tax point of view to use employed or self-employed staff in the business.

Exam focus

Exam kit questions on this area:
- Tetra
- Spike

Chapter 13

Starting in business

Key areas to consider for a new business scenario:

1 **Income tax**

   A **Badges of trade**

   = factors used to determine if an activity constitutes:

   - trading (s.t. income tax) or:
   - an investment (s.t. capital gains tax).

   • No single test conclusive.

   • Consider (SOFIRM): see table overleaf

   • Additional factors (FAST):
   - Finance method
   - Acquisition method
   - Similar Transactions

Exam focus

You need to be able to assess a given situation and express an opinion on whether it constitutes trading.

Exam kit questions on this area:

- Una
- Cate and Ravi

Test		Consider
Subject matter	S	• Type of good normally traded vs personal asset. • Income producing.
Ownership period	O	• Sale within short period indicates trading.
Frequency of transactions	F	• Repeated similar transactions indicate trading. • Single transaction may however constitute trading (e.g. toilet rolls case).
Improvements	I	• Work carried out to make asset more marketable may indicate trading.
Reason for sale	R	• Forced sale to raise cash indicates not trading.
Motive	M	• Intention to profit from transaction indicates trading. • Absence of profit motive does not prevent being deemed to be trading.

Remember: SOFIRM

B Trading income assessment

Exam focus

You are more likely to be given a tax adjusted trading profits figure in the question than have to calculate it at P6.

However you may have to calculate capital allowances. A reminder of the pro forma is given below

Chapter 13

Pro forma: Capital allowances computation

		Main pool	Special rate pool	Short life asset	Private use asset	Allowances
	£	£	£	£	£	£
TWDV b/f		X	X	X		
Additions not qualifying for AIA or FYA:						
Secondhand low emission cars (up to 75 g/km)		X				
Cars (76 – 130 g/km)		X				
Cars (over 130 g/km)			X			
Car with private use					X	
Additions qualifying for AIA:						
Special rate pool expenditure	X					
Less: AIA (Max £500,000 in total)	(X)					X
Transfer balance to special rate pool			X			
Plant and machinery	X					
Less: AIA (Max £500,000 in total)	(X)					X
Transfer balance to general pool		X				
Disposals (lower of original cost or sale proceeds)		(X)		(X)		
		X	X	X	X	X

Business tax

	£	General pool £	Special rate pool £	Short life asset £	Private use asset £	Allowances £
BA / (BC)				X / (X)		X / (X)
Small pools WDA						
WDA at 18%		(X)				X
WDA at 8%			(X)			X
WDA at 8%/18% (depending on emissions)					(X) × BU%	X
Additions qualifying for FYAs:						
New low emission cars (up to 75 g/km)	X					
Less: FYA at 100%	(X)					X
		Nil				
TWDV c/f		X	X	X		
Total allowances						X

The Annual Investment Allowance (AIA)

- Available to all businesses.
- 100% allowance for the first £500,000 of expenditure incurred in each accounting period of 12 months.
- Pro-rated for periods of account that are not 12 months.
- Available on acquisitions in the order:
  - special rate pool items
  - plant and machinery in main pool
  - short life assets
  - private use assets.
- **Not** available on cars
- Not available in the accounting period in which trade ceases.
- Expenditure above the maximum qualifies for WDA immediately.
- Taxpayer does not have to claim all / any of the AIA if he does not want to
- Any unused AIA is lost.

- The AIA must be split between related businesses.

  Businesses owned by the same individual is related where:
  - they are engaged in the same activities, or
  - share the same premises.

  In such circumstances the owner of the businesses can choose how to allocate a single AIA between them.

- Unrelated businesses owned by the same individual will each be entitled to the full AIA.

Writing down allowance (WDA)

- Available to all businesses.
- WDA available on a reducing balance basis.
- 18% in all pools except the special rate pool.
- Special rate pool WDA = 8%
- Pro rated for periods of account that are not 12 months.
- WDA adjusted for assets with private use by owner of business.

First year allowances (FYA)

- Available to all businesses
- 100% FYA available on:
  - new low emission cars ($CO_2 \leq 75$ g/km) (not available on any other cars), and
  - energy saving plant and machinery.
- Only available in the period of acquisition
- Never time apportion for short or long accounting periods.
- Taxpayer does not have to claim all/any of the FYA if he does not want to
- If any of the FYA is not claimed the balance is put in the main pool:
  - but not entitled to WDA until the following period.

Balancing adjustments

- Assets disposed of:
  - Deduct the sale proceeds from the relevant pool.
  - The amount deducted can never exceed the original cost of the asset.
  - A balancing adjustment may arise.

- A balancing charge (BC)
  - Can occur in any pool at any time
- A balancing allowance (BA)
  - Can occur in a 'single asset' column at any time
  - Only occurs on main pool or special rate when the business ceases to trade.

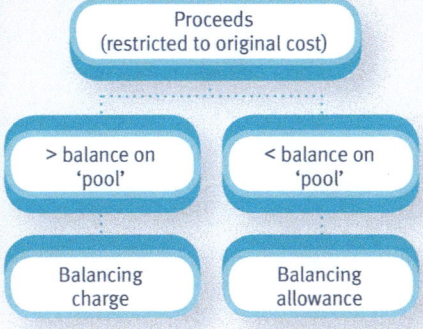

Summary of the capital allowances available for cars

CO_2 emissions

• Low emission:
   – Emissions ≤ 75 g/km
   – New = FYA 100%
   – Secondhand = as for standard emission cars

• Standard emission:
   – Emissions 76 – 130 g/km
   – Put in general pool
   – WDA 18% for a 12 month period

• High emission:
   – Emissions > 130 g/km
   – Put in special rate pool
   – WDA 8% for a 12 month period

• Private use cars
   – Separate column
   – WDA 18%/8% for 12 month period depending on emissions
   – BA or BC will arise on disposal

The special rate pool

- Pools expenditure incurred on:
  - long-life assets (LLA)
  - integral features of a building
  - thermal insulation of a building
  - high emission cars (CO_2 > 130 g/km)
- Pool operates in the same way as the general pool.
- AIA is available on new expenditure in this pool first (except high emission cars)
- WDA = 8% for a 12 month period, reducing balance basis.
- FYA is never available
- LLA = assets
  - with a working life ≥ 25 years, and
  - expenditure incurred ≥ £100,000 for a 12 month period (but not cars or P&M in a retail shop, showroom, hotel or office).

- Integral features
  = expenditure incurred on:
  - electrical (including lighting) systems
  - cold water systems
  - space or water heating systems
  - external solar shading
  - powered systems of ventilation, air cooling or air purification
  - lifts, escalators and moving walkways.
- Thermal insulation of a building
  = expenditure on thermal insulation on any commercial building (other than residential buildings in a property business)

Exam focus

Exam kit questions on this area:

- Liza

The small pool WDA

- Applies to the general pool and special rate pool only
  - can claim on either or both pools
  - claim is optional.
- Available where the balance on the pool after current period additions and disposals is ≤ £1,000
- WDA = any amount up to £1,000 for a 12 month period
- Pro-rated if period of account is not 12 months.

Short life assets (SLA)

- Each short life asset has its own column
- Short life means < 9 years useful life
- AIA available
- A balancing allowance or charge will arise when the asset is disposed of
- Beneficial where the asset with a short life is to be disposed of at less than TWDV
- Not available on motor cars
- If asset not disposed of within 8 years from the end of the accounting period in which it was acquired
  - the TWDV is transferred back into the general pool
- Election required for SLA treatment:
  - by first anniversary of 31 January following the end of the tax year in which the trading period, in which the asset was acquired, ends.

Chapter 13

Private use assets
(Unincorporated businesses only)

- Separate column for each private use asset
- Pool is:
  - written down by the AIA/WDA in full, according to the length of the accounting period, or FYA
  - but actual allowance claimed is restricted to business use proportion.
- BC/BA on disposal are also restricted to business use proportion.
- Cannot claim SLA treatment.
- Not applicable for companies.

Exam focus

Exam kit questions with plant and machinery allowances:

- Flame plc Group
- Liza
- Farina and Lauda
- Ziti
- Bond Ltd

Approach to computational questions

For P&M capital allowances, adopt the following step-by-step approach:

(1) Read the information in the question and decide how many columns / pools you will require.

(2) Draft the layout and insert the TWDV b/f (does not apply in a new trade).

(3) Insert additions not eligible for the AIA or FYAs into the appropriate column taking particular care to allocate cars into the correct column according to CO_2 emissions.

(4) Insert additions eligible for the AIA in the first column, then allocate the AIA to the additions.

Remember to time apportion if period of account is not 12 months.

Allocate the AIA to special rate pool additions in priority to additions of P&M in the general or other individual asset pools.

(5) Any special rate pool additions in excess of the AIA must be added to the special rate pool column to increase the balance available for 8% WDA.

Any general pool expenditure, in excess of the AIA, should be added to the general pool to increase the balance qualifying for 18% WDA.

(6) Deal with any disposal by deducting the lower of cost or sale proceeds.

(7) Work out any balancing charge / balancing allowance for single asset columns.

Remember to adjust for any private use if an unincorporated business (not relevant for companies).

(8) Consider if the small pools WDA applies to the general pool and / or the special rate pool.

(9) Calculate the WDA on each of the pools at the appropriate rate (18% or 8%).

Remember to:

- time apportion if the period of account is not 12 months
- adjust for any private use if an unincorporated business (not relevant for companies)

(10) Insert any additions of new low emission cars or energy saving P&M eligible for 100% FYA.

Remember the FYA is never time apportioned.

(11) Calculate the TWDV to carry forward to the next accounting period and add the allowances column.

(12) Deduct the total allowances from the tax adjusted trading profits.

Basis of assessment

Exam focus

You must know how adjusted trading profits are assessed to tax depending on whether the business is in its opening, ongoing or closing years.

New business – opening year rules

Year of assessment	Basis of assessment
First tax year (tax year in which trade starts)	Profits from date of commencement to following 5 April (Actual basis)
Second tax year	
(a) Period of account ending in the tax year is:	
(i) a 12 month accounting period	That period of account (CYB)
(ii) less than 12 months long	The first twelve months of trade
(iii) more than 12 months long	Twelve months ending as the accounting date in the second tax year (i.e. the last 12 months of the long period of account)
(b) No period of account ending in the tax year	Actual profits from 6 April to 5 April
Third tax year	Twelve months ending on the accounting date in the tax year (usually CYB, but if a long period of account = the last 12 months of that long period)
Fourth year onwards	Normal CYB

Choice of accounting date

The following table sets out the key points to consider and whether a year end late in the tax year (31 March) or early in the tax year (30 April) is the most advantageous in each case.

Accounting period end	31 March 2015	30 April 2015
Time lag between: earning income and paying tax	Assessed: 2014/15	Assessed: 2015/16
	April year end = profits assessed in following tax year, and tax paid 12 months later	
Time to submit computations	Submit: 31.1.2016 10 months to prepare	Submit: 31.1.2017 21 months to prepare
Overlap profits	None	11 months
Profits **increasing** in opening years, assessments based on:	Later (higher) profits	Earlier (lower) profits
Profits **decreasing** in opening years, assessments based on:	Later (lower) profits	Earlier (higher) profits

Business tax

Exam focus

As well as knowing the rules you may be required to consider tax planning aspects (e.g. choice of accounting date). Also need to consider the commercial needs of the business.

Exam kit questions on this area:

- Piquet and Buraco
- Jonny
- Tetra

2 VAT

- Compulsory registration.
- Voluntary registration.

See Chapter 14.

Exam focus

You may be required to determine when a business should register for VAT, identify advantages and disadvantages of registering earlier and penalties for late registration.

3 National Insurance Contributions (NIC)

- A sole trader has NIC liabilities based on his profits together with additional NIC liabilities if he employs staff.

Self-employed

Class 2
- Fixed at £2.80 per week.
- Payable on 31 January following the end of the tax year.

Class 4
- Paid on taxable trade profits less losses b/f.
- Rate of 9% of profits which fall between £8,060 and £42,385.
- Rate of 2% on profits which exceed £42,385.
- Paid at the same time as income tax under self-assessment.
- Not payable if over state pension age or under 16 at the **start** of the tax year
  - Note: upper age limit applies.

Key Point

Self-employed individuals who have employees pay:

- class 2 and class 4 NICs in respect of their unincorporated trade, and
- class 1 secondary and class 1A NICs in respect of earnings and benefits provided to employees.

Exam focus

Exam kit questions with NIC aspects:

- Tetra

Cash basis for small businesses

- Cash basis = calculating profits/losses on the basis of cash received and cash paid in the period of account (instead of normal accruals basis).
- Optional.
- Only available to unincorporated businesses (e.g. sole traders and partnerships) – not companies and LLPs
- Business must have annual turnover < VAT registration threshold (i.e. £82,000)
- Can continue to account on cash basis until annual turnover = 2 x VAT registration threshold (i.e. £164,000).

Exam focus

It should be assumed that the cash basis does **not** apply **unless** it is specifically mentioned in the question.

Under the cash basis:

- accounts can be prepared to any date in the year
- there is no distinction between capital and revenue expenditure re plant, machinery and equipment for tax purposes;
  - purchases are allowable deductions when paid for and
  - proceeds are treated as taxable cash receipts when an asset is sold.
- the flat rate expense deduction for car expenses (see below) will always be claimed instead of capital allowances in the P6 exam.

Advantages

- Simpler accounting.
- Profit taxed when realised and cash available to pay.

Disadvantages

- Losses can only be carried forward.

Flat rate expense deduction

Any unincorporated business (whether or not they are using the cash basis) can:

- opt to use flat rate expense adjustments
- to replace the calculation of actual costs incurred in respect of those expenses.

Exam focus

However in the P6 exam

- flat rate expenses will only be examined where the business has chosen the cash basis, and
- if the cash basis applies, the use of flat rate expenses will be assumed to also apply.

Type of expense	Flat rate expense adjustment
Motoring expenses	Allowable deduction = amount using the AMAP rates of 45p and 25p per mile (Note 1)
Private use of part of a commercial building (e.g. guest house)	Adjustment = fixed amount based on the number of occupants (Note 2). Covers: private use of household goods and services, food and utilities

Notes: If required:

1. AMAP rates are given in tax rates and allowances.
2. Fixed amount will be provided within the exam question.
   Private element of the other expenses (e.g. rent and rates) = adjusted for as normal.

Cessation of business

Exam focus

This scenario may be examined in the following circumstances:

- Sole trader sells his business to another sole trader.
- Sole trader sells his business to a company (incorporation of a business).
- Sole trader gifts his business.
- A partner leaves the partnership.
- Sole trader retires or dies.

Exam kit questions on this area:

- Mirtoon
- Spike
- Farina and Lauda
- Ziti

Consider the following taxes for each of the scenarios:

1. **Income tax**
   - Capital allowances:
     - Additions and disposals are allocated to relevant pools
     - No AIA/FYA/WDA given in final period
     - Compute balancing allowances (BA) or charges (BC)
     - If business transferred to connected person (i.e. business incorporated)
       - can elect to transfer at TWDV (no BAs or BCs)
   - Trading income assessment
     - Closing year rules:
       - Actual profit from the end of the basis period of the previous year until cessation
       - Deduct overlap profits

2 Capital gains tax

- Chargeable gains arise on disposal of assets (e.g. goodwill, property, investments).
- MV used as proceeds if assets gifted.
- Consider available reliefs:

Sale of business	Entrepreneurs' relief
	EIS/SEIS reinvestment relief
	Incorporation relief if sold to a company
	Rollover relief
Sale to company in exchange for shares	Incorporation relief
Gift of business	Gift relief

3 Inheritance tax

- Consider availability of business property relief on gift of an unincorporated business (Chapter 8)

Chapter 13

4 VAT

- Deregister when cease to make taxable supplies.

Situation	VAT position
Individual assets sold	Normal VAT rules apply (Chapter 14)
Assets held at date of cessation of trade	Deemed supply of business assets e.g. P&M, inventory, at MV at date of cessation (Deminimus limit £1,000)
Business transferred as going concern, and • Assets used in same kind of business as transferor, and • Transferee is or immediately becomes registered for VAT.	No VAT – not a taxable supply

Exam focus

Exam kit questions on this area:

- Mirtoon
- Jerome and Tricycle Ltd
- Ziti

Trading losses

Be prepared to apply your knowledge to a particular scenario, compare alternative strategies and explain your recommendations.

Trading losses
- Calculated in the same way as a trading profit.
- Trading income assessment is nil.

Relief against total income
- Available in:
  - tax year of the loss and/or,
  - preceding tax year

- Offset can not be restricted to preserve PA.
- Offset is restricted if loss exceeds maximum amount (see below).
- Excess loss is automatically carried forward or can be set against chargeable gains.

Relief against chargeable gains
- Available in the same years as a claim against total income:
  - tax year of the loss, and/or
  - preceding tax year
- Only possible after a claim against total income has been made in the tax year in which a claim against gains is required
- Do not need to claim against total income in both years first
- No maximum restriction.

- Trading loss is treated as a current year capital loss
- Deducted
  - after the offset of current year capital losses
  - before capital losses brought forward, and
  - before the AEA.

Relief against future trading profits

- Relieved against:
  - the first available
  - trading profits only
  - of the same trade.
- Loss offset cannot be restricted.

Order of offset

When there is more than one loss to offset:

- deal with the earliest loss first
- losses b/f are offset in priority to CY and PY claims.
- watch out for the maximum restriction (if applicable) (see below)

Reduced capital allowances claim

- Loss arising can be reduced by **not** claiming full capital allowances.
- The TWDV c/f for CAs will be correspondingly higher.
- Higher CAs will therefore be claimed in the future rather than creating or increasing a loss now.

Opening years relief

In addition to reliefs available for an ongoing business, special opening year loss relief is available.

- A loss incurred in any of the **first four tax years** of a new business can be set against:
  - total income
  - of the three tax years preceding the year of the loss
  - on a FIFO basis.
- One claim covers all three years.
- Offset cannot be restricted to preserve PA.
- Maximum restriction applies as for ongoing loss relief against total income.

Terminal loss relief

In addition to standard relief against total income and chargeable gains, special terminal loss relief is available.

Relief is given for the loss of the **last 12 months** of trading.

- Relief is:
  - against profits of the same trade
  - of the tax year of cessation, and
  - the three preceding tax years
  - on a LIFO basis.
- Calculation of the terminal loss:
  (1) loss from 6 April to date of cessation
  (2) plus proportion of loss in the preceding tax year up to 12 months prior to cessation date
  (3) plus unrelieved overlap profits.

Business transferred to company

- Business transferred to company.
- In exchange wholly/mainly for shares (80% of consideration).
- Trading losses at date of cessation carried forward indefinitely provided owner retains shares.
- Offset against future income received from company **in any order**:
  - earned income (salary, bonus)
  - interest
  - dividends.

Maximum deduction from total income

Maximum deduction from total income
= **greater of**:
- £50,000, or
- 25% of adjusted total income (ATI).

Therefore restriction will be £50,000 unless ATI exceeds £200,000.

Adjusted total income (ATI):

	£
Total income	X
Less: Gross PPCs	(X)
ATI	X

Key Point

The maximum restriction may be beneficial as it could avoid wasting PAs.

Maximum deduction limit:

- applies to trading losses set against:
  - current year total income
  - earlier years **if** set against income other than profits of the same trade.
- does not apply to losses set against chargeable gains.

Offset against earlier years:

- set against profits from same trade first, then non-trading income
- no restriction to offset against profits from same trade
- restrict offset against non-trading income
- loss that cannot be set off = not lost
  - can claim to offset against chargeable gains, or
  - c/f as usual

Procedure for dealing with questions involving losses

(1) Determine tax adjusted loss/profits after capital allowances for each period of account.

(2) Determine when loss relief is available (i.e. in which tax years).
   - Different options if in opening/ ongoing/ closing years.

(3) Layout IT computations for tax years side by side.
   - Leave spaces to insert losses offset.

(4) Set up a loss working for each loss to show how it is utilised.

(5) If more than one loss
   - Consider in chronological order.

(6) Consider options available depending on whether early year, last year, chargeable gains in tax year.

(7) Offset losses in most beneficial way:
   - Obtaining relief at highest rates of tax.
   - Taking relief as soon as possible.
   - Not wasting personal allowances.

Watch out for the maximum deduction rules.

Exam focus

Exam kit questions on this area:
- Mirtoon
- Jonny
- Spike
- Kantar
- Jodie

Choice of loss reliefs

- Objectives in choosing the most appropriate loss claim:
  - obtain relief at the highest marginal tax rate
  - obtain relief as early as possible
  - avoid wasting PAs (and the AEA for CGT where appropriate).
- Relief against total income and the opening year relief give earliest relief, rather than carrying the loss forward.
- A large gain in a single year (the year of loss or year immediately preceding):
  - indicates a claim against chargeable gains may be beneficial
  - but must relieve total income of same year first and maximum restriction may apply
  - may result in wastage of PAs
  - maximum restriction does not apply against gains
  - relief against gains is at 10%, 18% or 28%.
- Relief against total income and the opening year relief are optional reliefs but carry forward relief is mandatory and automatic if no specific claim is made.
- No partial claims allowed (i.e. all or nothing reliefs).
- Losses can be restricted by making reduced capital allowance claims.
- Relief against total income applies to two years but separate claims are required for each year and such claims can be made in either order.
- The best claim may be a compromise of the main objectives (e.g. may accept lower tax saving if relief is given earlier).

Partnerships

Treat like sole traders – each partner is the owner of the business

Step 1	Determine the tax adjusted accounting profit/loss after capital allowances of the partnership for each accounting period.
Step 2	Allocate these profits or losses between the partners according to the **profit sharing agreement** (PSA) in the **accounting period**. If PSA requires a salary or interest on capital allocation: • treat as a share in their trading profits The balance of profits or losses: • shared in the profit sharing ratio (PSR). **If a partner joins or leaves during the accounting period:** • treat as if a change in PSR • time apportion profits, apply appropriate PSA to each part.
Step 3	Determine the taxable trading income assessment for the tax year or the loss reliefs available for each partner using their share of the accounting profit/loss. **Partner joins – opening year rules** **Partner leaves – closing year rules** **Other years – normal CYB basis** (i.e. assess the profits of 12 months to a/c date)

Exam focus

Exam kit questions on this area:
- Tetra
- Farina and Lauda

Self-assessment for the self-employed

Tax Year	Due Date for paying the tax	Consequences of paying tax late
Opening year	• Income tax and class 4 NICs = due on the 31 January following the tax year • If 2015/16 = first tax year of trading, due by 31 January 2017 • Filing date = same date	• Late payment interest at 3% for each day payment is late • Additional penalty of at least £100 is levied for late filing of return (see Chapter 11)
Second year and thereafter	• Income tax and class 4 NICs = payable in three instalments • If 2015/16 = second or subsequent year: Payment on account 1: – due 31 January 2016 (i.e. 31 January in tax year of assessment) Payment on account 2: – due 31 July 2016 (i.e. 31 July following tax year of assessment) Balancing payment: – due 31 January 2017 (i.e. 31 January following tax year of assessment)	• Late payment interest at 3% for each day payment is late • Additional penalty of at least £100 is levied for late filing of return • If the balancing payment is late: – as above, plus extra penalties of at least 5% of the amount due will apply (see Chapter 11)

chapter 14

Value added tax

In this chapter

- Introduction.
- Types of supply.
- VAT registration.
- Deregistration.
- VAT returns.
- Output VAT.
- Input VAT.
- Special accounting schemes.
- Disaggregation.
- Land and buildings.
- Partial exemption.
- Capital goods scheme.
- VAT administration.
- VAT penalties.

Value added tax

Exam focus

VAT can be examined in the context of companies or an unincorporated business.

The new topics introduced at P6 are popular topics, but retention of all F6 is also essential as all areas can be tested.

Introduction

- VAT is an indirect tax charged on consumer spending.
- VAT is charged on:
  - a taxable supply
  - by a taxable person
  - in the UK
  - in the course or furtherance of a business.
- Output tax: charged on sales.
- Input tax: incurred on purchases and expenses.

Types of supply

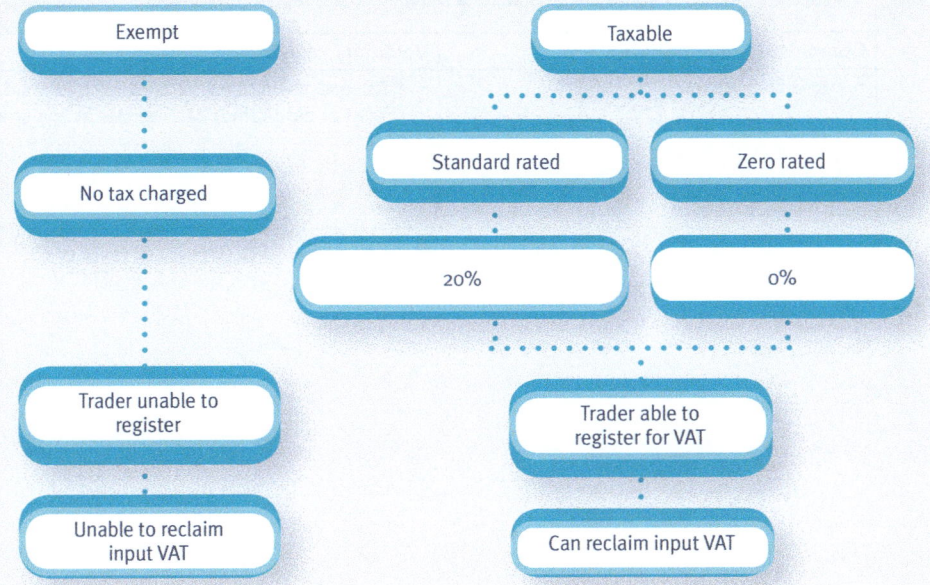

VAT registration

- A taxable person is someone who is, or is required to be, registered for VAT.

Compulsory registration	Voluntary registration

- Required when:
  - value of taxable supplies (standard or zero-rated)
  - exceeds the registration threshold (i.e. £82,000).
	- Traders making taxable supplies (standard rated or zero-rated) can register at any time.

Compulsory registration

Historic turnover test	Future test
• Taxable supplies in the last 12 months exceed £82,000. • Perform test at the end of each month. Inform HMRC: • Within 30 days of the end of the month in which the threshold is exceeded. Registered from: • End of month following the month in which the threshold was exceeded or • An agreed earlier date.	• Taxable supplies in the next 30 days is likely to exceed £82,000. • Perform test constantly. • By the end of the 30 day period in which the threshold is expected to be exceeded. • From the start of the 30 day period.

Exam focus

Exam kit questions on this area:

- Ash
- Kantar
- Sprint Ltd and Iron Ltd

Voluntary registration

Advantages	Disadvantages

• Input tax recoverable.
• If making zero-rated supplies:
   – VAT returns will show VAT repayable
   – can register for monthly returns to aid cashflow.
• Avoids penalties for late registration.
• May give the impression of a more substantial business.
	• Output charged on sales:
	   – if make standard rated supplies to customers who are not VAT registered will be an additional cost to them
	   – may affect competitiveness.
	• VAT administration burden.

Exam focus

Exam kit questions on this area:

- Ash

Deregistration

Compulsory deregistration	Voluntary deregistration
• When cease to make taxable supplies.	• If value of expected taxable supplies in the next 12 months will not be > £80,000.
Inform HMRC:	
• within 30 days of ceasing to make taxable supplies.	• At any time when above test satisfied.
Deregistered from:	
• date of cessation, or	• Date of request for deregistration, or
• an agreed earlier date.	• An agreed later date.

- Consequences of deregistration
  - Deemed to make a supply of business assets held at date when cease to be a taxable person (e.g. capital items, trading inventory)
  - Exclude items if no input tax reclaimed on them (e.g. cars purchased with private use)
  - No output charge if VAT on deemed supply is ≤ £1,000.

Value added tax

Exam focus

Exam kit questions on this area:
- Mirtoon
- Jerome and Tricycle Ltd
- Jodie

VAT returns

- Normally quarterly.
- If receive VAT repayments can elect for monthly returns.
- VAT payable
  = (Total output tax less total input tax).
- A businesses must:
  - file the return online, and
  - pay electronically,
  - within one month and seven days of the end of the VAT period
- VAT inclusive amounts:
  - VAT
    = Gross amount x 20/120 (or 1/6)
  - Net amount
    = Gross amount x 100/120 (or 5/6)

Output VAT

Value of supply

- Consideration in money:
  - Trader's VAT exclusive selling price less the amount of any trade or bulk buy discounts offered.
- If a prompt payment discount is offered, VAT is charged on the amount received.
- Consideration not in money or money and something other than money:
  - Open market value.
- Gifts of inventory and non-current assets
  - Replacement value.
- Certain gifts are not taxable supplies:
  - goods which cost ≤ £50 per customer, per year, and
  - any number of business samples, and
  - gifts of service (to employees or customers).
- Goods for own use
  - Replacement value if purchased for business purposes (no output VAT if purchased for private purposes).

Relief for impairment losses

- Relief available where:
  - output VAT in respect of an outstanding debt has been accounted for and paid by the supplier
  - the supplier has written the debt off in the accounts as irrecoverable
  - six months has elapsed since the debt was due for payment.
- Claim the relief as input VAT on the VAT return.
- Customers who have not paid for goods/services within 6 months of the due date must repay the input tax they have previously claimed.

Value added tax

Transfer of a going concern (TOGC)

- Transfer of a business is not treated as a supply for VAT purposes, therefore:
  - no output VAT charged on assets transferred by seller
  - no input VAT recoverable by purchaser.
- Conditions (all must be satisfied):
  - business transferred as a going concern
  - no significant break in trading
  - to a taxable person (VAT registered or liable to become VAT registered)
  - same type of trade carried on after the transfer.
- A building on which an option to tax has been made cannot be part of the TOGC
  - unless the purchaser also opts to tax the building.
- Transferee may:
  - take over VAT registration of the transferor, but
  - also inherits the transferor's VAT liabilities.
- Where there is a transfer of a business which is not a going concern, or where the transferee is not a taxable person:
  - VAT is payable on the individual assets transferred.

Exam focus

Exam kit questions on this area:

- Jerome and Tricycle Ltd
- Ziti

Input VAT

- Conditions to reclaim input VAT:
  - Must be taxable person when incurred (exception = pre-registration VAT).
  - Supply must have been to the person making the claim.
  - Supply must be properly supported, normally by VAT invoice.
  - Goods/services must be used for business purposes.
- No distinction between capital and revenue expenditure.
  - Input VAT is recoverable on the purchase of capital assets as well as revenue expenditure.

Non-deductible VAT

- Business entertainment
  - includes hospitality of any kind (e.g. food, drink, accommodation)
  - excludes staff entertainment, and entertaining overseas customers.
- Motor cars
  - Purchase – only recoverable if used 100% for business.
  - Leasing – if partly used for private purposes, only 50% of VAT on leasing charge recoverable.
  - Motor expenses – provided some business use, 100% recoverable.
  - If input VAT is not recovered on purchase, output VAT is not charged on the disposal.

Value added tax

- Fuel – Input tax 100% deductible even if private fuel provided

  Output VAT chargeable on:
  - fuel reimbursed in full
    - amount reimbursed
  - not reimbursed in full
    - fuel scale charge (based on CO_2 emissions).
    - scale charge will be provided in exam.
  - Private use
    - input VAT cannot be claimed on goods or services not used for business purposes
    - an apportionment is made for partial private use.
  - Goods for own use
    - input VAT recoverable if purchased for business purposes (not recoverable if purchased for private purposes).

Key Point

Where VAT is not recoverable on capital expenditure (e.g. purchase of a car) capital allowances are claimed on the VAT inclusive cost.

Pre-registration input VAT

Conditions to reclaim input VAT:

Goods	Services
• Acquired in the 4 years before registration, and • Still held at date of registration	• Supplied in the 6 months before registration

Special accounting schemes

- Three special schemes aimed at small businesses.

Cash accounting scheme

Operation	Conditions	Advantages
• VAT accounted for on cash payments and cash receipts	• Taxable turnover ≤ £1,350,000 • VAT payments and returns must be up to date • Must leave the scheme if taxable turnover > £1,600,000	• Do not pay output tax until receive payment from customer • Provides automatic relief for irrecoverable debts

Exam focus

Exam kit questions on this area:
- Drench, Hail Ltd and Rain Ltd

Value added tax

Flat rate scheme

Operation	Conditions	Advantages
• Flat rate of VAT applied to total turnover (including exempt supplies and VAT) • Flat rate determined by trade sector • Flat rate only used to simplify preparation of VAT return – still need to issue tax invoices	• Taxable supplies for the next 12 months ≤ £150,000 • Businesses are eligible to stay in the scheme until their annual income exceeds £230,000	• Reduces administration – do not need to account for VAT on individual purchases • May reduce total VAT payable

Exam focus

Exam kit questions on this area:

- Bamburg Ltd

Annual accounting scheme

Operation	Conditions	Advantages
<ul><li>One VAT return prepared a year</li><li>Return due: 2 months after end of annual VAT period</li><li>Payments on account (POA): – 9 POA due in months 4 – 12 – each POA is 10% of VAT for previous year</li><li>Balancing payment due with the VAT return on same date</li><li>New businesses base POA on estimated VAT liability</li></ul>	<ul><li>Taxable turnover ≤ £1,350,000</li><li>VAT payments and returns must be up to date</li></ul>	<ul><li>Reduces administration</li><li>Regular payments can help cashflow</li></ul>

Value added tax

Disaggregation

- Where HMRC are satisfied that persons are carrying on separate activities which could properly be regarded as a single business, they will issue a direction
- The direction will state that the persons named in therein are carrying on activities listed together (i.e. a partnership is deemed to exist).
- A direction cannot have retrospective effect.

Land and buildings

Types of supply

Supplies of land and buildings in the UK can be either be zero-rated, standard-rated or exempt.

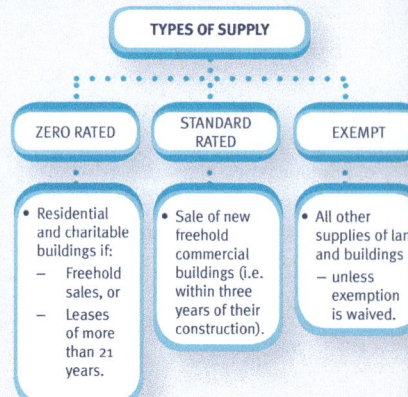

Opting to tax

A VAT registered vendor or lessor of a building can opt to waive the exemption of the building. This is usually referred to as 'opting to tax.'

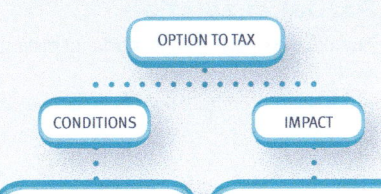

OPTION TO TAX

CONDITIONS
- Election must be filed within 30 days of signing.
- Can be withdrawn within initial six month cooling off period or after 20 years otherwise irrevocable.
- Election cannot be made for a part of a building, although the election can be made separately for each property owned.

IMPACT
- Supply becomes a taxable supply.
- Input tax in respect of the building can be recovered.
- Future supplies of the building (e.g. sales or rents, must be standard-rated).
- New owners are not bound by a previous owner's election, except for transfers within a VAT group (Chapter 16).

Exam focus

Exam kit questions on this area:
- Janus plc Group
- Flame plc Group
- Ziti

Partial exemption

Traders who make both taxable and exempt supplies:

- only part of the input tax is recoverable.

Exam kit questions on this area:

- Janus plc Group
- Spetz Ltd Group
- Nocturne Ltd

Methods of determining recoverable input tax

The standard method for determining the amount of recoverable input VAT is as follows

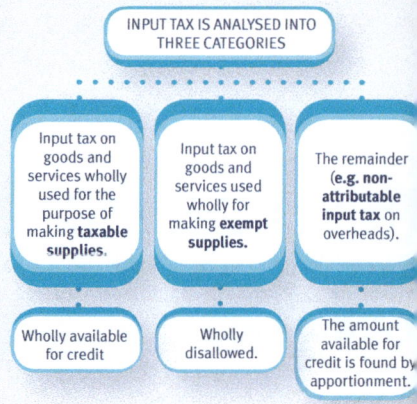

Chapter 14

- Non-attributable input VAT reclaimable:

$$\frac{\text{Total taxable supplies (exc. VAT)}}{\text{Total supplies}} = \%$$

  - Exclude supplies of capital goods
  - Round % up to next whole number
  - Any other reasonable method of apportionment can be agreed with HMRC

- Can either calculate the reclaimable % each quarter or can use last year's %

Annual adjustment

- Recalculate recoverable % at the end of each accounting period based on actual supplies for the year.
- Any under or over-claim accounted for in first VAT return of next year, or can bring forward to final VAT return for this period.

De minimis limits

- All input tax (including that relating wholly or partly to exempt supplies) may be recovered if the business is below the de minimis limits.
- Three tests to see whether a business is de minimis:

  (1) **Total input tax ≤ £625 per month** on average, and
  Value of **exempt supplies ≤ 50%** of value of **total supplies**

  (2) **Total input tax less input tax directly attributable to taxable supplies ≤ £625 per month** on average, and
  Value of **exempt supplies ≤ 50%** of value of **total supplies**

  (3) **Input tax relating to exempt supplies ≤ £625 per month** on average, and
  Input tax relating to exempt supplies ≤ 50% of total input VAT

Value added tax

- Only need to satisfy one test.
- If business was de minimis last year:
  - can provisionally recover all VAT this year (unless input tax expected to be > £1million).
- Status must be reviewed at end of the accounting period based on whole year.
- Annual adjustment made as above, if necessary.

Annual test

- The business can apply the de minimis tests once a year rather than every return period if:
  - the business was de minimis in the previous year, and
  - the annual test is applied consistently throughout the current year, and
  - the input VAT for the current year is not expected to exceed £1 million.

- This means that the business can provisionally recover all input VAT relating to exempt supplies in each return period without having to perform de minimis calculations.
- At the end of the accounting period, the de minimis status must be reviewed based on the year as a whole and an annual adjustment made if necessary.

Capital goods scheme

- Applies to partially exempt traders who spend large sums on land and buildings or computer equipment.
- Initial deduction of input tax is made in the ordinary way and then reviewed over a set adjustment period.

- Assets covered by the scheme:

Item	Value	Adjustment period
Land and buildings	£250,000 or more	10 years (5 years where subject to a lease of less than 10 years at acquisition)
Computers and computer equipment	£50,000 or more	5 years

A trader making say 70% taxable supplies and 30% exempt supplies:

- can initially reclaim 70% of the input VAT charged in respect of a building
- adjustments are made over the next 10 (or 5) years if the proportion of exempt supplies changes.

The annual adjustment is:

$$\frac{\text{Total input tax}}{\text{10 or 5 years}} \times (\text{\% now} - \text{\% in the original year})$$

Disposal of building in adjustment period

- normal annual adjustment
- further adjustment

if disposal:	for remainder of adjustment period assume
taxable	100% taxable use
exempt	0% taxable use

Exam focus

Exam kit questions on this area:

- Janus plc Group
- Bond Ltd
- Hyssop Ltd

Value added tax

VAT administration

VAT records

- Must keep records of all goods/services received and supplied, sufficient to allow the return to be completed and allow HMRC to check the return.
- Retain records for 6 years.
- Type of records to retain:
  - copies of VAT invoices issued
  - record of outputs (e.g. sales day book)
  - evidence to support recovery of input tax
  - VAT account.

VAT penalties

- **Standard penalties** apply in the same way for income tax, CGT, corporation tax and VAT
- depends on the behaviour of the taxpayer (see Chapter 11).
- Errors in VAT returns can give rise to
  - Default interest, and
  - Standard penalty for the submission of an incorrect VAT return

Specific penalty relating to VAT

- the default surcharge

Default surcharge

Arises	• Return submitted late, or
	• VAT paid late
First default	• HMRC serve a surcharge liability notice
	• Specifies a surcharge period:
	– ending 12 months after the end of the VAT period to which the default relates
Further defaults	• Surcharge period extended to 12 months after the end of the VAT period in which the latest default relates
	• If default involves late payment of VAT – Surcharge penalty levied

Surcharges	Default in surcharge period	% of VAT unpaid
	First	2%
	Second	5%
	Third	10%
	Fourth and more	15%

Note:

- Surcharge assessments at rates below 10% will not be issued for amounts of ≤ £400.
- Where rate is 10% or more, the minimum surcharge is £30.

Value added tax

Error on VAT returns

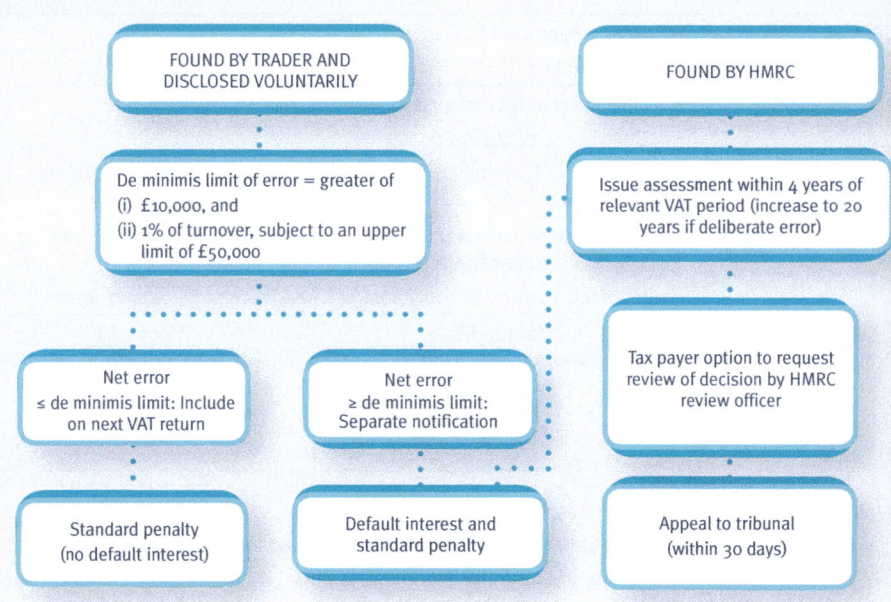

Default interest

Arises	- HMRC raise an assessment to collect undeclared/overclaimed VAT.
	- Voluntary disclosure of errors exceeding de minimis limit.
Charged	- From due date of payment to actual date of payment.

Value added tax

chapter

15

Corporation tax
– liability and losses

In this chapter
- Chargeable accounting periods.
- Taxable total profits computation.
- Corporation tax payable.
- Trading profits – specific issues for companies.
- Capital allowances.
- Long period of account.
- Self-assessment.
- Penalties.
- Trading losses – single company.
- Restriction of carry forward of losses.
- Non-trading losses.

Corporation tax – liability and losses

Exam focus

Corporation tax is very important.

Questions on corporation tax will regularly feature in the exam and you need to be able to prepare a corporation tax computation, as well as explain the tax implications of company transactions.

This chapter revises the key issues in preparing a corporation tax computation, summarises the self-assessment rules and sets out the options for a single company making losses.

Chargeable accounting periods (CAPs)

- Corporation tax computation required for each CAP.
- Cannot be longer than 12 months.
- Starts:
  - When start to trade.
  - Previous CAP ends.
- Ends:
  - 12 months after start
  - end of period of account (i.e. company's period for which it draws up accounts)
  - cease to trade/be resident in UK
  - go into administration/liquidation.

Taxable total profits computation

ABC Ltd
Corporation tax computation for year ended 31 March 2016

	Notes	£
Trading profits	(a)	X
Interest income	(b)	X
Overseas income	(c)	X
Property business profit		X
Net chargeable gains	(d)	X
Total profits		X
Less: QCD relief	(e)	(X)
Taxable total profits (TTP)	(f)	X

Corporation tax payable

- Tax liability:

	£
TTP × 20%	X
Less: DTR	(X)
CT payable	X

Notes

(a) Trading profit = Adjusted trading profit less capital allowances. Adjustments include interest and royalties paid for trade purposes.

(b) Interest income includes on non-trading loan relationships (i.e. interest receivable and payable).

(c) Overseas income may include rental income, interest income and branch profits, but excludes overseas dividends.

(d) Net chargeable gains
= capital gains less all capital losses:

- Indexation allowance (IA) to date of disposal using:

$$\frac{\text{RPI @ date of disposal} - \text{RPI @ date of acquisition}}{\text{RPI @ date of acquisition}}$$

- rounded to 3.d.p
- cannot create or increase a capital loss
- if there is a fall in the RPI between acquisition and disposal: IA = £Nil
- no AEA
- consider rollover relief and substantial shareholding exemption.

(e) Qualifying charitable donations (QCDs)

- includes all charitable donations by company which are not allowed as a trading expense.

(f) Dividend income from UK and overseas companies is never chargeable to corporation tax and not included in TTP.

However, is included as FII to determine the augmented profits for instalment purposes.

Trading profits – specific issues for companies

- Loan relationships
- Goodwill and other intangibles
- Patent box
- Research and development
- Gains on shares of companies

Loan relationships

All income, expenses, capital and revenue arising from loans is taxed under the loan relationship rules.

	Trading loan	Non-trading loan
Example	Loan notes issued to raise funds to acquire P&M	Loan to acquire investment property or a subsidiary
Income/ capital profit	Trading income	Interest income
Expense/ capital loss	Deduct from trading income	Deduct from interest income. Relief available for net loss

Exam focus

Exam kit questions on this area:

- Banger Ltd and Candle Ltd
- Helm Ltd Group

Corporation tax – liability and losses

Goodwill and other intangibles

Intangibles (excluding goodwill)

- Intangible assets acquired by companies are not capital assets for capital gains purposes, but follow accounting treatment.
- Debits and credits, income and capital = part of trading income assessment
- A company can claim a 4% WDA p.a. if no amortisation in financial accounts or amortisation rate is < 4% p.a.
- On sale of intangibles:
  - profit or loss is assessable/deductible for trading purposes.
- Accounting profit or loss will give rise to an identical tax profit or loss:
  - unless the 4% election is made
  - in which case a tax adjustment must be made by comparing the accounting profit to the taxable profit.

Goodwill

- The treatment of goodwill differs from other intangible assets.
- Amortisation or impairments of goodwill are disallowable for corporation tax.
- Profit/loss on disposal = proceeds less cost (as book value for tax = cost)
  - Profit on disposal = taxable as part of trading profits.
  - Loss on disposal = relieved as a non-trading debit.

Special intangibles rollover relief

- If a new intangible is acquired:
  - within 12 months before or up to 36 months after
  - part of the taxable credit may be deferred.
- Applies to goodwill and other intangibles

Chapter 15

- Maximum deferral is:

	£
Lower of	
– Proceeds	
– Amount reinvested	X
Less: Cost of original intangible	(X)
	X

Exam focus

Exam kit questions on this area:
- Janus plc Group
- Cinnabar Ltd

Patent box relief

Scheme for companies owning / holding patents for the purposes of their trade.

Can elect for

- profits relating to those patents
- to be taxed at a lower rate of corporation tax.

Profits relating to patents will be taxed at:

- 10% by FY2017
- but scheme is being phased in over 5 years
- in FY2015, 80% of the profits in the 'patent box' will be taxed at effective 10% rate.

Method of relief:

- reduce taxable trading profits by:

80% x net patent profit x (main rate – 10%) / main rate

Corporation tax – liability and losses

Scheme is:

- optional
- must be claimed within **two years** of the end of the accounting period in which the patent profits arise
- applies to **all profits derived from patents:**
  - royalty income, and
  - a proportion of the profits made on goods or services where a patent has been used in the underlying production process.

Research and development expenditure (R&D)

- Expenditure on R&D as defined by GAAP qualifies for certain reliefs for companies.
- Expenditure includes
  - Staffing costs
  - Agency staff
  - Materials, water, fuel and power
  - Software
  - Subcontractor payments

Exam focus

Exam kit questions on this area:

- Bond Ltd

Exam focus

Exam kit questions on this area:

- Sank Ltd and Kurt Ltd
- Cinnabar Ltd

- Relief as follows:

Small and medium sized company	Large company
+ 130% allowable	+ 30% allowable, or Claim alternative tax credit (see below)
Repayment = 14.5% × lower of: • trading loss • 230% of qualifying R&D expenditure	No repayment option for losses.
	Claim enhanced relief for contributions to qualifying bodies (e.g. charities and universities who carry out the R&D).

Alternative 'above the line tax credit' for large companies

Large companies can:

- Opt to claim a tax credit against their corporation tax liability = 11% of the qualifying R&D expenditure
- Method of relief:
  - deducted from the CT liability, and
  - include as taxable income in TTP (taxed at 20%)
- Net benefit of 8.8%
  - instead of 6% if the 30% extra deduction claimed.
- If no CT liability or insufficient liability to net off all the tax credit the excess will be:
  - paid in cash, net of tax
  - up to max = PAYE/NIC liability for R&D employees for CAP

Corporation tax – liability and losses

- if repayable tax credit > max cash repayment allowed:

  the remaining tax credit can be:

- carried forward and set against the first available future CT liability, or
- group relieved.

Key Point

Until 1 April 2016, companies can claim 30% extra deduction or the alternative tax credit relief. Thereafter, only the alternative tax relief will be available.

Gains on shares for companies

Substantial shareholding exemption

- Disposal of shares out of a substantial shareholding (SSE) = exempt from corporation tax.
- Substantial shareholding = where company has owned:
  - ≥ 10% interest in the shares
  - for ≥ 12 months continuously
  - in the last 2 years.
- If shares held < 12 months exemption still applies if:
  - shares disposed of are in a new company, and
  - trade and assets of another 75% group company are transferred to that new company prior to sale of shares, and
  - trade and assets have been owned by group for ≥ 12 months in last 2 years.

Exam focus

Exam kit questions on this area:
- Janus plc Group
- Opus Ltd Group
- Helm Ltd Group
- Sprint Ltd and Iron Ltd
- Cinnabar Ltd

If SSE does not apply

Gains on shares for companies

- If disposal not out of a substantial shareholding:
  - use matching rules for companies, and
  - calculate a gain.
- The matching rules for company disposal of shares is:
  - Same day acquisitions
  - Acquisitions in the previous nine days (FIFO basis)
  - Acquisitions from the share pool.
- Calculation of gains
  - No IA given on same day acquisitions and purchases in previous 9 days.
  - IA is available on share pool shares.

The share pool

The share pool for companies is different to the share pool for individuals as follows:

- it contains shares in the same company, of the same class, purchased up to 9 days before the date of disposal.
- The pool keeps a record of the:
  - number of shares acquired and sold
  - cost of the shares, and
  - indexed cost of the shares (i.e. cost plus indexation allowance)
- The pool cost and the indexed cost will be provided in the exam
- When shares are disposed of out of the share pool, the appropriate proportion of the cost and indexed cost which relates to the shares disposed of is calculated on an average cost basis (as for individuals).

Capital allowances

The changes to the capital allowances regime for unincorporated businesses apply equally to companies, with the following additional points:

(1) The AIA must be split between related companies.

Companies owned by the same individual will be regarded as related where they:

- are engaged in the same activities,
- or share the same premises.

In such circumstances the owner of the companies can choose how to allocate a single AIA between them.

This could be the case if an individual runs two companies from home, the AIA will be spilt between the two businesses.

Unrelated companies owned by the same individual will each be entitled to the full AIA.

(2) For capital allowance purposes, only one AIA is available to a group of companies.

Note that:

- A 'group' for this purpose is defined by the Companies Act and essentially applies where a parent company holds a simple majority shareholding (> 50%) in another company or companies at the end of the accounting period.

When allocating the AIA:

- the group members can allocate the maximum £500,000 AIA in any way across the group
- the AIA does not have to be divided equally between them
- all of the allowance can be given to one company, or any amount can be given to any number of companies within the group.

Exam focus

Exam kit questions on this area:

- Sank Ltd and Kurt Ltd

(3) The 8% special rate of WDA in respect of plant and machinery that is integral to a building applies to both initial and replacement expenditure.

Replacement expenditure occurs where more than 50% of an asset is replaced in a 12-month period.

This prevents a tax deduction being claimed for the repair of such assets where such repairs are substantial and the asset can be used in the trade.

Previously, a deduction was allowed for repairs expenditure, on an asset if it could be used in the trade before the 'repairs' were carried out.

This deduction is no longer available for plant and machinery integral to a building; instead tax relief is spread via the special rate WDA.

(4) Expenditure on energy saving or environmentally beneficial plant and machinery qualifies for a 100% FYA.

Where a company has made a loss:

– it may surrender that part of the loss that relates to such allowances in exchange for a payment from HMRC
– payment = 19% of the loss surrendered.

Such a claim can only be made where the company is unable to use the losses in the current accounting period against:

– its own profits, or
– via group relief.

The claim is made in the company's corporation tax return.

The maximum payment that a company can claim is the higher of:

- £250,000 and
- its total PAYE and NIC liabilities for the relevant accounting period.

Where any of the qualifying plant and machinery is sold within four years of the end of the relevant accounting period:

- there will be a claw-back of an appropriate part of the payment made, and
- a reinstatement of the loss.

Long period of account

Accounting period > 12 months must be split into two CAPs:

- First 12 months
- Remainder

For each CAP, HMRC require:

- a separate CT comp, and
- a separate CT600 return

Note there will be:

- Two separate pay days (i.e. 9 months after end of CAP)
- But only one file date of the returns (i.e. 12 months after end of long period of account).

Corporation tax – liability and losses

Splitting the profits:

Tax adjusted trading profit before capital allowances	Time-apportion
Capital allowances	Separate computations (where the CA is less than 12 months, the WDA/AIA is reduced accordingly but not FYA)
Interest/Property/Other income	Compute accrued amount for each period separately (Note)
Chargeable gains	According to date of disposal
Qualifying charitable donations	According to date paid

Note: if information to apply the strict accruals basis is not available, then time apportion

Self-assessment

Payment date • Normal date • Large company (see below)	• 9 months after end of CAP • 4 quarterly instalments: on 14th of months 7, 10, 13 and 16 after start of CAP • Based on estimated liability for the year • Payments must be reviewed and revised as necessary at each instalment date. • A company will not be required to make quarterly instalments in two circumstances: (1) CT liability < £10,000 (2) Company not large in previous CAP, and augmented profits ≤ £10 million (÷ number of related 51% group companies and/or reduced for short CAP)
Payment method	• Payment must be made electronically
Filing date	• 12 months after end of period of account • Must be filed electronically along with copies of accounts • Must be filed using Inline eXtensible Business Reporting Language (iXBRL)

Corporation tax – liability and losses

Late payment interest Repayment interest	• Charged from due date • Earned from date paid • Charges and receipts are interest income/expense under the loan relationship rules
Retention of records	• 6 years from end of CAP
Group payment arrangements	• Optional • Where at least one group company pays instalments • Related 51% group companies can arrange for one group company to pay quarterly instalments on behalf of group • Can save interest as overpayments effectively netted off against underpayments • Each company must still prepare separate corporation tax computation at end of CAP.

Large companies

- Large companies must pay corporation tax by instalments (see table above)
- A company is large if its augmented profits for the CAP > £1.5 million threshold:
  - short CAP – time apportion threshold
  - related 51% group companies – divide by total number of related companies at end of previous CAP.

Augmented profits

	£
TTP	X
Franked investment income (FII)	X
Augmented profits	X

- FII = (dividends received from UK and overseas companies) x 100/90
- Exclude dividends from 51% group companies

Corporation tax – liability and losses

Exam focus

Exam kit questions on this area:
- Sank Ltd and Kurt Ltd

Compliance checks

- HMRC must give written notice of their intention to commence a compliance check (enquiry) into a tax return.
- The time limit to make a compliance check:

  Where a return is submitted on time:
  - 12 months after the actual submission date

  Where a return is submitted late:
  - 12 months after 31 January, 30 April, 31 July or 31 October following the actual filing date of the return.

- A compliance check ends when HMRC give notice
- Company has 30 days to amend the return, if applicable.

Exam focus

Exam kit questions on this area:
- Sank Ltd and Kurt Ltd

Chapter 15

Amendments, errors and mistakes

- A company may amend its return:
  - within 12 months from the filing date
- HMRC may amend a return:
  - within 9 months from the date the return is filed
- A company may make a claim for overpayment relief:
  - within four years from the end of the relevant accounting period.

Personal liability of senior accounting officers

- Designated senior accounting officer of large companies and groups have to:
  - ensure the companies' accounting systems = adequate
  - certify annually that the accounting systems are adequate, or
  - specify the inadequacies and confirm that the auditors have been informed
- Large = turnover of more than £200 million and/or a total of more than £2 billion on the statement of financial position.
- Penalties (personal and corporate) can be levied for careless or deliberate failure of these obligations

Exam focus

Exam kit questions on this area:

- Janus plc Group

Corporation tax – liability and losses

Penalties

Standard penalties

- same rules for income tax, corporation tax, CGT, VAT and NIC (see Chapter 11).

Other penalties for corporation tax

Offence	Penalty
Failure to keep and retain required records.	Up to £3,000 per accounting period.
Late filing of corporation tax return: - Within 3 months of filing date - More than 3 months after filing date Additional penalties: - 6-12 months after filing date - More than 12 months after filing date	- Fixed penalty = £100 (Note) - Fixed penalty increased to £200 (Note) - Additonal 10% of tax outstanding 6 months after filing date - Additonal penalty increased to 20% Note: Fixed penalties rise to £500 and £1,000 if persistently filed late (i.e. return for 2 preceding periods also late)

Trading losses – single company

Summary of reliefs

Carry forward	Current year relief	Carry back relief
		Current year offset first then carry back 12 months
<ul><li>Offset against:<ul><li>First available</li><li>Trading profits</li><li>Of same trade</li></ul></li><li>Indefinite carry forward</li></ul>	<ul><li>Offset against<ul><li>Total profits (income and gains)</li><li>Before QCD relief</li></ul></li><li>Carry forward any remaining losses</li><li>Must offset maximum amount possible if claimed</li><li>QCD relief is lost if no profits to offset against</li><li>Optional claim</li></ul>	

Corporation tax – liability and losses

Trading loss pro forma

	2014	2015	2016
	£	£	£
Trading profit	X	Nil	X
Less: Loss b/f	–	–	(X)3
	X	Nil	X
Other income	X	X	X
Net chargeable gains	X	X	X
Total profits	X	X	X
Less: Loss relief			
– Current year		(X) 1	
– Carry back	(X)2		
	Nil	Nil	X
Less: QCD relief	Wasted	Wasted	(X)
Taxable total profits	Nil	Nil	X

Key Point

2015 is the loss-making year. The trading profit assessment in this year is nil.

Keep a separate working of the loss and how it is utilised.

Assuming there is sufficient loss available, and assuming that the loss is being relieved as early as possible, the order in which to off-set the loss is as follows:

(1) Current year relief; in the year the loss is made
(2) Prior year relief; carrying available losses for offset back 12 months
(3) Future year relief; against trading profits only.

Exam focus

Use the loss pro forma to help you adopt a methodical approach to a question involving trading losses.

Show your workings in a loss working summarising how the loss has been offset.

Corporation tax – liability and losses

Approach to loss offset

(1) Lay out years – columnar form.
(2) Calculate TTP ignoring losses.
(3) Choose loss relief by reference to:
  - cashflow
  - offset as soon as possible
  - carry back may result in a repayment of tax
  - carry forward will only result in a reduction of future tax
  - wastage of QCDs
    - unrelieved amounts cannot be carried forward.
(4) Use separate loss working.
(5) If more than one loss, deal with earliest first.

Exam focus

Exam kit questions on this area:
- Drench, Hail Ltd and Rain Ltd
- Janus plc Group
- Bond Ltd
- Opus Ltd

Terminal loss relief

- Loss in final 12 months of trading
    - current year offset; then
    - carryback against total profits (before QCD relief)
    - of 3 years preceding loss making period
    - on a LIFO basis.

Restriction of carry forward of losses

- Cannot carry forward losses beyond the date of a change in ownership (> 50% shares) where:
    - a negligible trading activity is revived after a change in ownership, or
    - change in ownership and a major change in the nature of trade in a 3 year period.

Corporation tax – liability and losses

Non-trading losses

NON-TRADING LOSSES

CAPITAL LOSSES

- Current year then carry forward
- Against chargeable gains only

- Partial claims are not allowed.
- Losses must be offset as soon as possible.

PROPERTY INCOME LOSSES

- Current year then carry forward
- Against total profits before QCD relief

LOAN RELATIONSHIP DEFICITS

Four options available:
- against total profits before QCD relief of the current period.
- carry back against interest income of the previous 12 months (36 months if the company is ceasing to trade).
- carry forward against non-trading profits of future periods
- group relief

- Partial claims are allowed.
- The company can therefore choose how much of the deficit is relieved under each option.
- Claims for current period and carry back relief must be made within two years of the end of the AP of loss.

chapter 16

Groups – corporation tax and value added tax

In this chapter

- Group relationships.
- Group relief.
- Consortium relief.
- Capital gains groups.
- Sales of shares or assets.
- Transfer of trade within 75% group.
- Transfer pricing.
- VAT group registration.

Groups – corporation tax and value added tax

Exam focus

Questions on groups can be examined in the compulsory or optional section of the paper.

There has been a large corporation tax groups scenario on almost every P6 exam so far.

Group relationships

Relationship	Definition
Related 51% group companies	- One company directly or indirectly owns > 50% of another, or - Both are 51% subsidiaries of a third company.
Group relief (GR) group	- A parent company and all its direct and indirect 75% subsidiaries (see below). - The definition of 75% subsidiary is extended for GR purposes only. In addition to owning 75% of the share capital (SC) the parent must also be entitled to receive 75% of profits and 75% of assets on winding up.
Capital gains group	- A parent company (principal member (PM)) and its 75% subsidiaries (see below) and their 75% subsidiaries – provided PM has $\geq$ 50% effective interest in subsidiary. - A 75% subsidiary of a PM cannot be a PM itself (i.e. a company can only be a member of one gains group).
75% subsidiary	- One company owns $\geq$ 75% of SC of another, or - Both are 75% subsidiaries of a third company. - Includes direct/indirect holdings. - Definition includes overseas companies.

Relationship	Definition
Consortium owned company	• ≥ 75% ordinary SC owned by companies, each owning ≥ 5% and • Each member entitled to ≥ 5% profits and ≥ 5% net assets • Excludes a company that is 75% subsidiary of another.

Illustration – Group relationships

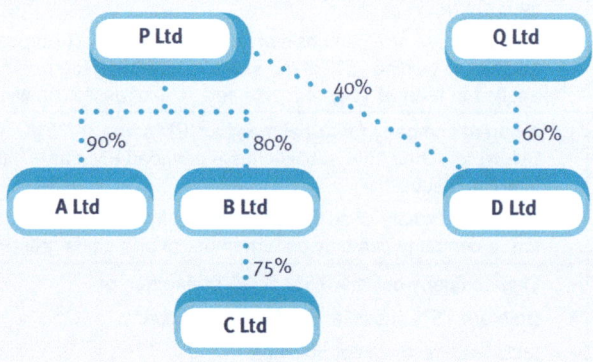

Relationship	Group members
Related 51% group companies of P Ltd	• A Ltd, B Ltd and C Ltd • D Ltd excluded as < 50%
Group relief (GR) group	• P Ltd, A Ltd, B Ltd • C Ltd is not part of the group as P Ltd's interest is < 75% i.e. interest in C Ltd = 60% (80% × 75%) • B Ltd and C Ltd form a separate losses group
Capital gains group	• P Ltd, A Ltd, B Ltd and C Ltd • C Ltd is part of the gains group as it is a 75% subsidiary of a 75% subsidiary and P Ltd's effective interest (60%) is > 50%
Consortium relief group	• D Ltd is a consortium company of P Ltd and Q Ltd • D Ltd is owned ⩾ 75% by companies and each consortium member (P Ltd and Q Ltd) is entitled to ⩾ 5%

Key Point

You must be clear on the distinction between a group relief group and a capital gains group.

Groups – corporation tax and value added tax

- Related 51% group companies include:
  - Both UK and overseas resident companies
  - Companies leaving group
- Exclude:
  - Dormant companies (if dormant for whole CAP)
  - Non-trading holding company
  - Companies joining the group
- The number of related companies is based on the position at the end of the previous CAP, hence the treatment of companies joining/leaving in the period.

Effect of related 51% group companies:

Effect:
- Divide the threshold by the number of related companies to determine whether instalments are necessary.
- Dividends from related companies (UK and overseas) = not FII
- One AIA allocated between group companies
- VAT group registration available
- Group payment arrangement available if at least one company pays by quarterly instalments.

Chapter 16

Group relief (GR)

- Transfer losses between any member of a GR group.
- Group definition:
  - includes overseas companies
  - but the relief can only be claimed by UK companies, or UK branches of overseas companies.
- Exceptions:
  1. Overseas losses can be group relieved to UK parent if
     - EEA resident subsidiary or has a branch in EEA, and
     - losses **cannot** be relieved elsewhere.
  2. Losses of a UK branch can be group relieved in the UK to a UK company if
     - UK branch is owned by an EEA company, and
     - losses have not been utilised elsewhere

Exam focus

Exam kit questions on this area:

- Janus plc Group
- Drench, Hail Ltd and Rain Ltd
- Cinnabar Ltd
- Opus Ltd
- Sprint Ltd and Iron Ltd

- Rules:

Surrendering co.	Claimant co.

• **Any amount** of **current year**:
  – trading loss
  – debits on non trading loan relationships,
 	
plus **excess**:
  – QCD relief
  – UK property losses
  – expenses of management.
	Maximum claim: £
	TTP (a) X
	Less: CY losses (b) (X)
	                                  X
	
	(a) TTP is after deduction of losses b/f and QCD's
	(b) The company's own losses are taken into account in computing the maximum claim, but need not actually be claimed before GR

- Watch for:
  - non-coterminous CAPs
    - GR restricted to common CAP (profits/losses deemed to accrue evenly)
  - companies joining group
    - GR only available for losses arising whilst in the group
  - companies leaving group
    - GR only available for losses arising whilst in group, but
    - No GR once arrangements for sale are in place.

Due date for group relief claim

- 12 months after the claimant company's filing date for the CAP covered by the claim (i.e. usually 2 years after the end of the CAP).

Payment for group relief

- The claimant company may pay the surrendering company for the loss.
- Any such payment for the group relief is ignored in both companies' CT computations.

Consortium relief

- Two or more companies owning
  - Together ≥ 75% or another company and
  - Individually ≥ 5%
  - No one company owns ≥ 75%
  - UK companies only, but overseas companies can help to meet the definition.
- Similar to group relief but:
  - Losses to surrender:
    - between consortium company (CC) and UK members only (i.e. not between members)
    = lower of:
      - member's TTP / trading loss
      - (member's % holding in CC) × CC's TTP / trading loss

Exam focus

Always consider whether or not any of the companies in the question form a consortium

Exam focus

Exam kit questions on this area:

- Janus plc Group
- Cinnabar Ltd

Capital gains groups

1 Transfer of assets within group

- Automatically take place at no gain/no loss (NG/NL) regardless of the price paid.
- Transferee company takes over asset at cost plus indexation to date of transfer.
- Degrouping charge where transferee company leaves the gains group still owning the asset, within 6 years of the NG/NL transfer
  - calculated as gain that would have arisen, using MV as proceeds, at date of NG/NL transfer
  - degrouping charge is added to the consideration received by the vendor company selling the shares in the company leaving the group.
  - unlikely to be taxable as company selling the shares is likely to benefit from substantial shareholding exemption on disposal of the shares.
  - group ROR not available for a degrouping gain.

Exam focus

Exam kit questions on this area:

- Drench, Hail Ltd and Rain Ltd
- Janus plc Group
- Helm Ltd Group

2 Reallocation of gains

- A joint election can be made to reallocate chargeable gains or allowable losses when an asset is sold outside the group.
- The election enables:
  - group chargeable gains and allowable capital losses to be offset
  - thus maximising the use of capital losses.

Key Point

Current year chargeable gains or allowable losses can be transferred, but not brought forward losses.

3 Rollover relief (replacement of business assets)

- For ROR purposes, all companies within a capital gains group are treated as carrying on a single trade
  - gain in one company can be rolled into the acquisition by another group company
  - group ROR not available for a degrouping gain.

Exam focus

Exam kit questions on this area:

- Liza
- Opus Ltd
- Flame plc Group
- Sprint Ltd and Iron Ltd
- Bond Ltd
- Helm Ltd Group

4 Pre-entry losses

- On joining a gains group
  - identify capital losses (realised losses only).
- Can only use against:
  - gains on own assets held at date of joining group
  - gains on new assets acquired from outside group for use in business.
- Can not be used against gains of other group companies.

5 Intangible assets

- Similar rules exist for transfer of intangible assets between group members (i.e. tax neutral).
- Degrouping charge if transferee company leaves group within 6 years.
- Degrouping charge can be allocated to another group member.

6 Stamp taxes

- Assets subject to stamp duty and stamp duty land tax can be transferred between group members as an exempt transfer.
- If the transferee company leaves the group within 3 years the duty is payable.

Approach to a groups question

- AIM = to allocate gains and all losses for the benefit of the group (i.e. to save as much tax as possible).
- The approach (as a general rule) should be as follows:
  (i) Prepare a diagram of the group structure.
  (ii) Determine the number of associated companies, 75% group(s) and consortia.
  (iii) Set up a tabular pro forma for TTP and Augmented profits (if relevant). May need to calculate gains, consider ROR and reallocation of gains to calculate TTP.
   Do this **before** dealing with losses.
  (iv) Complete to TTP, separating out any losses to loss memoranda.
  (v) Determine the best use of any qualifying losses to save tax as soon as possible.
  (vi) Where there are a number of losses in a question, deal with the losses with the most restricted set off first.
  (vii) Compute CT liability on revised TTP.
  (viii) Show CT payable and any losses or surpluses to be carried forward.
- Also consider alternatives:
  - carrying back (after current period relief) as an alternative to GR, as this can generate a repayment, and
  - the effect of DTR; surrender of losses must not waste DTR.
  - try to reduce the TTP of companies exceeding the threshold; this will be beneficial to the group cash flow as CT instalments will no longer be required.

Sale of shares or assets

Sale of shares:

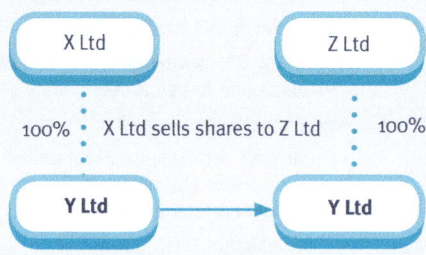

X Ltd

- Gain/loss on disposal of shares unless SSE available.
- Possible degrouping charge: add to disposal proceeds for sale of shares.
- Still include Y Ltd as a related company as it is based on the previous CAP.

Y Ltd

- Carries on trading.
- Group relief stops when arrangements in place: time apportion if mid-year.
- Trading losses c/f may be subject to restriction as Y Ltd has changed owners
- Pre entry capital losses cannot be used against gains on Z Ltd's assets.
- Related to X Ltd until the next CAP.

Z Ltd

- Related to Y Ltd from the next CAP.
- Group relief starts when Y Ltd joins: time apportion if mid-year.
- Pay stamp duty 0.5%

Exam focus

Exam kit questions on this area:

- Helm Ltd Group

Sale of assets:

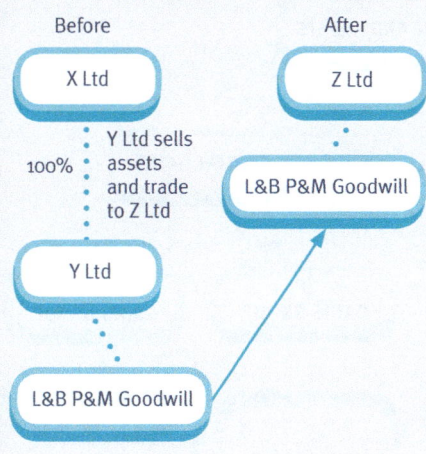

X Ltd

- No effect.

Y Ltd

- Ceases trading: end of CAP.
- Gains/losses on disposal of chargeable assets (e.g. land and buildings).
- Trading profit/loss on disposal of goodwill.
- Possible ROR for gains/profit on goodwill.
- BA/BC on plant and machinery.
- Losses remain in Y Ltd: possible terminal loss relief.
- VAT: transfer of going concern.

Z Ltd

- Acquires assets at MV.
- Capital allowances for plant and machinery based on MV.
- Pay stamp duty on land and buildings 0-4%.

Transfer of trade within a 75% group

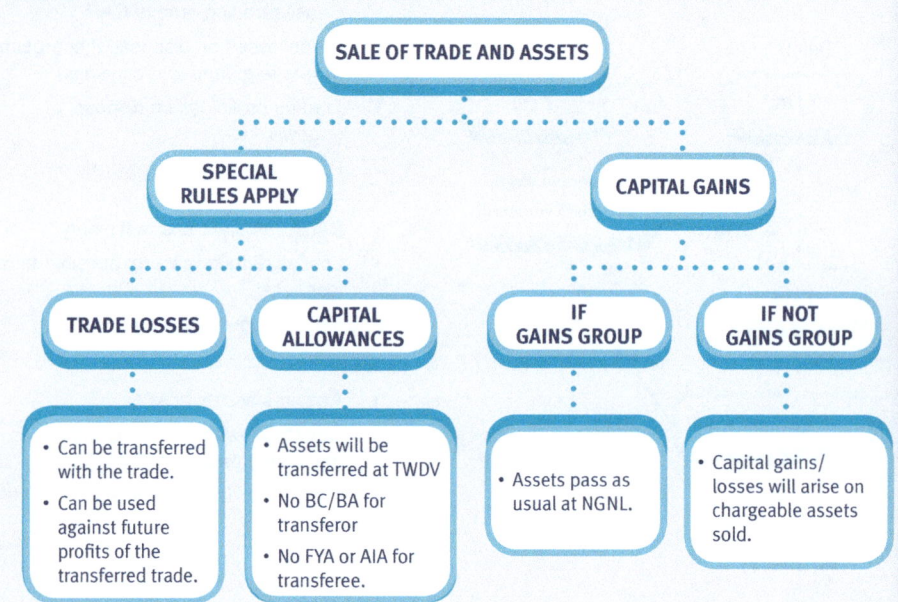

Transfer pricing

- Applies where transactions between group companies, which have not taken place at an arms length price, result in a tax advantage (e.g. decreased profits, increased losses) to a UK company.
- The advantaged company must increase its taxable profits to reflect an arm's length price.
- The other company can reduce its taxable profits by a corresponding amount if it is UK resident.
- Rules only apply where the companies involved are large (or medium sized under limited circumstances).
- Rules do apply if:

  Large → any company
  S/M → overseas company in non-qualifying territory
  (e.g. no DTR agreement)

- Rules do not apply if:

  S/M → UK S/M

  S/M → overseas company in qualifying territory
  (e.g. DTR agreement exists).

VAT Group registration

- Membership
  - voluntary
  - by any UK companies under common control.
- Consequences
  - Representative member responsible for accounting for VAT
  - No VAT on intra-group sales
  - Only one VAT return to prepare
  - All members jointly/severally liable for VAT
  - Limits for cash accounting scheme applied to whole group
  - Other VAT schemes for small businesses not available.

Exam focus

Be prepared to explain whether or not a company should be included in a VAT group.

- Special consideration required for:
  - company making zero-rated supplies
  - exclude if in monthly repayment position to maintain cash flow advantage
  - companies making exempt supplies
    - inclusion in group will make the group partially exempt.

Exam focus

Exam kit questions on this area:

- Liza
- Sprint Ltd and Iron Ltd

chapter 17

Overseas issues – corporation tax and value added tax

In this chapter

- Company residence.
- UK company operating overseas.
- Branch exemption election.
- Overseas income – computational approach.
- Controlled foreign companies.
- Overseas aspects of VAT.

Overseas issues – corporation tax and value added tax

Exam focus

Overseas issues are likely to feature as part of a question and is likely to be included within a groups question.

Company residence

Definition

A company is resident in the UK if it is:

- **incorporated** in the UK, or
- incorporated outside the UK and
  - its place of **central management and control** is situated in the UK.

Exam focus

Exam kit questions on this area:
- Spetz Ltd Group

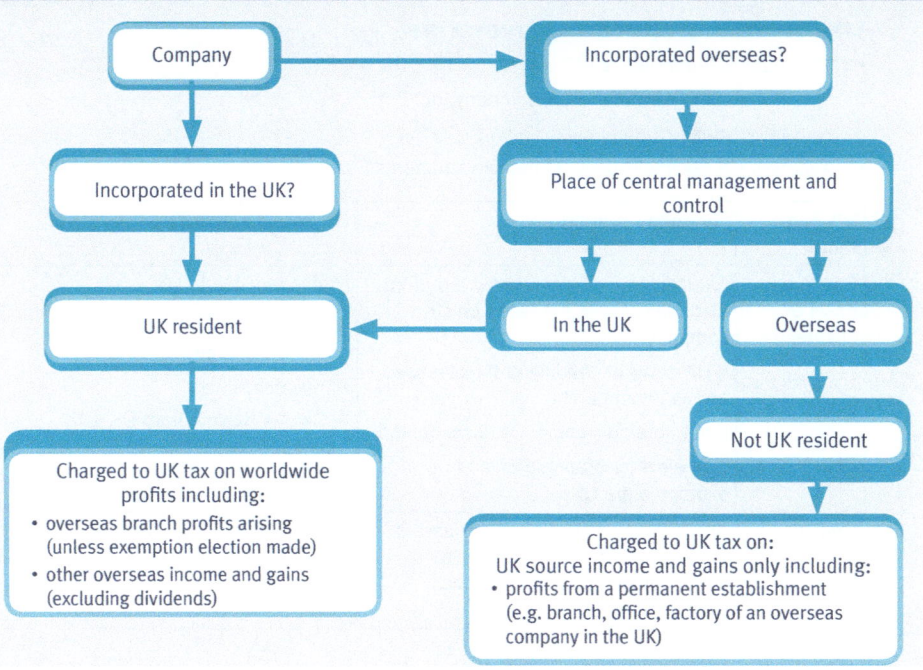

UK company operating overseas

- Can establish operations in 2 ways:
  - a branch/division of the UK company, or
  - an overseas resident subsidiary.
- Different UK tax implications of the two structures.

UK Tax factor	Overseas branch	Overseas subsidiary

Scope and basis of charge	Extension of UK operations; therefore all profits arising assessed on UK company.
	
	If UK control – trading profit assessed as UK trading profit.
	
	If not, foreign income (i.e. local control).
	
	Can elect for branch profits to be exempt in the UK.
		Profits remitted to UK
		• as interest/property income:
		  – is chargeable to UK CT
		• as dividends:
		  – is exempt from UK CT

Capital allowances	Available on overseas located assets purchased and used by overseas branch unless election for branch exemption made.	Not available under UK tax rules.

UK Tax factor (contd)	Overseas branch (contd)	Overseas subsidiary (contd)
Trading loss relief	Can relieve trading losses against UK profits. No relief if election for branch exemption made. Can use UK losses against profits of overseas branch.	No UK trading loss can be surrendered to overseas subsidiary. Subsidiary in EEA can surrender loss to UK parent if no alternative relief. Branch in UK of an EEA company can surrender losses to UK if not relieved in another country.
Chargeable gains	Capital gains computed using UK rules (i.e. ROR is available on reinvestment and capital losses can be utilised).	UK rules not applicable.
Impact on tax rates	None – as **not** a separate entity.	Related company: • Reduces the threshold for determining whether instalments are required. • If dividend received from overseas related company = ignored as not FII. • If dividend received from overseas non related = included as FII.

Overseas issues – corporation tax and value added tax

Exam focus

Exam kit questions on this area:

- Spetz Ltd Group

Branch exemption election

- Can be made at any time
- Effective from start of CAP after election made
- Irrevocable
- Applies to all overseas branches

Effect

- Profits = exempt in UK
- Losses = no relief in UK
- No capital allowances
- Capital gains = not taxable in UK

Tax planning

- May be beneficial not to make election if

    (i) DTR means little or no UK CT payable, and/or

    (ii) losses possible or anticipated in an overseas branch in the future.

Overseas income – computational approach

(1) Calculate the gross amount of overseas income for inclusion in computation of TTP.

	£
Foreign income received	A
Add: WT = A × $\frac{\% \text{WT}}{100 - \%\text{WT}}$	X
	X

(2) Compute the CT liability on the TTP.

(3) Offset DTR

For each source of overseas income lower of:
- overseas tax suffered, and
- UK tax on overseas income.

(4) Unrelieved overseas tax on branch profits only

Relief may be available via:
- carry back
- carry forward.

Key Point

Offset QCD relief and losses against UK income to maximise DTR.

Exam focus

Exam kit questions on this area:
- Banger Ltd and Candle Ltd
- Spetz Ltd Group

Controlled foreign companies (CFCs)

Exam focus

Always consider the possibility of an overseas company being a CFC

- Provisions exist to prevent UK companies setting up overseas subsidiaries and accumulating profits in countries with lower rates of tax.

Definition

A non-UK resident company

- Controlled by UK resident companies, and/or individuals
- that has artificially diverted profits from the UK.

Key Point

The usual rule of taxing only non-dividend income from an overseas subsidiary and exempting dividend income does not apply to a CFC.

CFC charge to UK corporation tax

- A CFC charge applies if:
  - **UK company owns ≥ 25%** interest in the CFC
  - the CFC has chargeable profits.
- CFC charge is:

	£
(UK company's share of CFC profits x 20% of CT) (see Note)	X
Less: Creditable tax	
DTR that would be available if CFC were UK resident	(X)
UK CT on income of CFC that is taxable in UK (if any)	(X)
Income tax suffered by the CFC on its income	(X)
CFC charge	X

Note: UK company's share of CFC profits

= **apportioned based on the % of shares held**

- UK companies self assess their liability to the CFC charge.
- A clearance procedure exists to check how the rules will be applied.

No CFC charge

- CFC charge does not arise if
  - no chargeable profits of CFC
  - an exemption applies
  - the shareholder = an individual.

No chargeable profits of CFC

- **Chargeable profits** = income of CFC (not chargeable gains) that are artificially diverted from the UK, calculated using the UK tax rules.
- CFCs = regarded as having **no chargeable profits** (and therefore no CFC charge) if:
  - the CFC does not hold assets or bear any risks
    - that are managed in the UK, or are
    - under tax schemes intended to reduce UK tax, or
  - the CFC would continue in business if the UK management of its assets and risks were to cease.

Exemptions to CFC charge

- CFC may have chargeable profits, but no CFC charge as it satisfies one of the exemptions:

Exempt period	The first 12 months of the company coming under the control of UK residents
Excluded territories	HMRC provide a list of approved territories where rates of tax are sufficiently high to avoid a CFC charge arising.
Low profits	The CFC's TTPs are: • ≤ £500,000 in a 12-month period – of which ≤ £50,000 comprises non-trading profits.
Low profit margin	The CFC's accounting profits are ≤ 10% of relevant operating expenditure.
Tax exemption	The tax paid in the overseas country is ≥ 75% of the UK CT which would be due if it were a UK resident company.

Exam focus

Exam kit questions on this area:

- Klubb

Overseas aspects of VAT

EU transactions for supply of goods

	'Destination system'	'Origin system'
Status of parties	Supplier and customer VAT registered (Business to business) (B2B)	Supplier registered, customer not registered (Business to individual)
Rate of VAT	Country of origin • zero-rated Destination country • rate applicable in destination country	Country of origin • rate applicable in country of origin
Supplier	No VAT	Account for output tax May have to register in country of destination if supplies exceed threshold
Customer	Pays output VAT based on date of acquisition, which is the earlier of: • date of invoice • 15th day of month following month goods came into UK Claims VAT suffered as input tax	Cannot recover VAT as not registered

Non-EU transactions for supply of goods

Imports

- Importer pays VAT at point of entry into UK.
- Can pay monthly through Duty Deferment System.
- Recovers VAT suffered as input tax.
- Net effect is the same as for purchases from the UK.

Exports

- All goods are zero-rated.

Key Point

All supplies of goods within or outside the EU = taxable supplies.

Issue = whether the supply is zero or standard rated.

It will never be an exempt supply.

Net effect on purchases from within or outside the EU = same, unless purchaser makes exempt supplies.

Supply of services

VAT is generally charged in the place of supply.

Supply of services to	Place of supply
Business customer	Where the customer is established
Non-business customer	Where the supplier is established

Overseas issues – corporation tax and value added tax

These rules can be applied to a UK business as follows:

UK business		Accounting for VAT
Supplies services to	• Overseas business customer (B2B)	• Place of supply is overseas. • Outside the scope of UK VAT.
	• Overseas non-business customer	• Place of supply is UK. • Output VAT charged at standard UK rate.

Receives services from	• Overseas business (B2B)	• Place of supply is UK.
		• Reverse charge procedure:
		  – UK business accounts for 'output VAT' at standard UK rate on VAT return.
		  – This VAT can then be reclaimed as input VAT.

Chapter 17

Time of supply for cross border supply of services

- For single supplies:
  - tax point = earlier of
    (i) when the service is completed, or
    (ii) paid for
- For continuous supplies:
  - tax point = end of each billing or payment period

Exam focus

Exam kit questions on this area:

- Janus plc Group

Overseas issues – corporation tax and value added tax

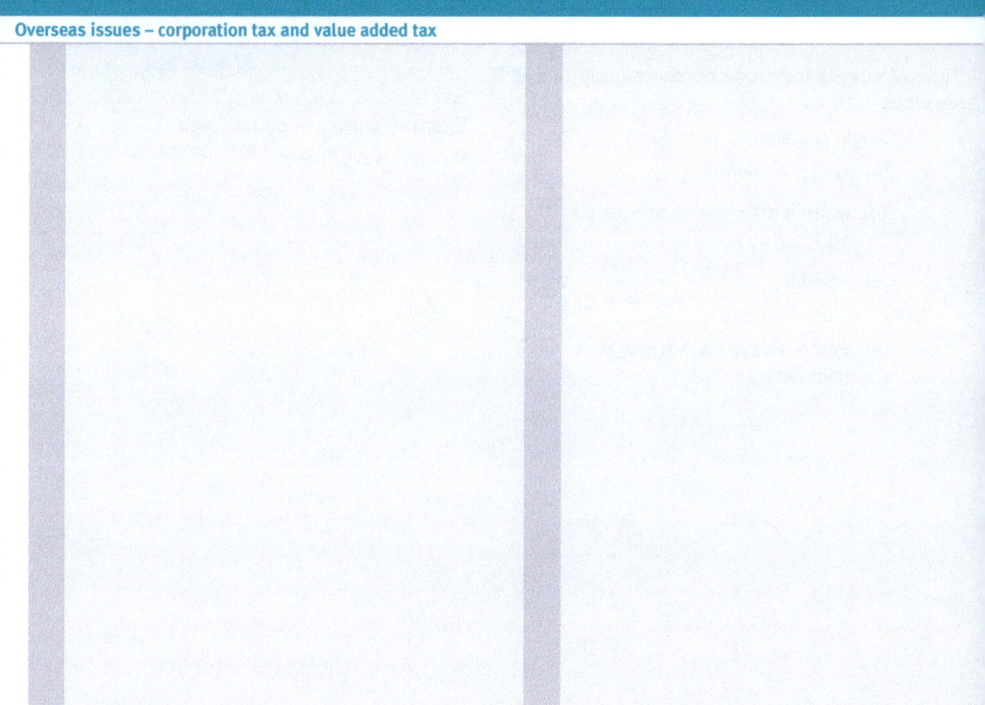

chapter

18

Business finance and tax planning for companies

In this chapter

- Long term finance.
- Short term finance.
- Financing non-current assets.
- Business vehicle.
- Extracting profits from a business.
- Incorporation of a business.
- Disincorporation.
- Close companies.
- Personal service company.
- Withdrawing investment.
- Tax planning for companies.

Long term finance

Debt versus Equity

	Equity	Debt
Maximum amount	• Specified in Articles of Association	• No limit
Return on investment	• Dividends • Only paid if profitable	• Interest • Paid regardless of profitability
Corporate investors	• Dividends received = exempt	• Interest received = taxable
Individual investors	• Basic rate taxpayer = no further liability • Higher rate / additional rate taxpayer = dividend upper rate element payable	

Other points	• If not listed:
	  – difficult to issue new shares
	• Owner managed businesses:
	  – do not like control to be diluted
	  – usually issue shares to existing shareholders or family members
		• lender may require security (i.e. a charge over company assets)

Incentives to issue shares

For individuals:
- SEIS relief.
- EIS relief.
- VCT relief.

For companies:
- Substantial shareholding exemption.

Short term finance

- Bank overdraft.
- Short term loans.
- Trade credit.
- Invoice discounting.
- Debt factoring.
- Hire purchase and leasing.

Financing non-current assets

	Outright purchase	Hire purchase	Leasing
Initial outlay	• Full cost	• Instalment	• Lease rental
Subsequent cost of purchase	• None	• Instalments spread over length of HP agreement • Includes HP interest	• Lease rentals spread over length of lease • Includes finance charge
Tax relief against profit	• Capital allowances available	• Interest = allowable deduction against profit • Capital allowances available	• Lease rental and depreciation = allowable deduction against profit (other than high emission cars with CO_2 > 130 g/km where 15% of lease charge is disallowed) • No capital allowances
VAT recoverable? (except cars)	Yes	Yes	Yes
Sale proceeds on disposal	Yes	Yes	No

Chapter 18

Business vehicle

Sole trader versus company

	Sole trader	Company
Taxation of profits	• Current year basis • Assessed to income tax • Based on taxable trading profits • Adjustments for private use • Personal allowance may be available • Taxed at 20%, 40% or 45% • Class 2 NICs • Class 4 NICs	• Accounting period basis • Assessed to corporation tax • Based on taxable total profits • Taxable total profits = after individual's employment income deducted • No adjustments for private use • No personal allowance • Taxed at 20% • No NICs on business profits • Individual assessed to income tax and class 1 NICs on employment income

Business finance and tax planning for companies

	Sole trader (contd)	Company (contd)
Relief for losses	• Available against personal income of individual • Against total income of current and/or previous tax year • Extension claim against chargeable gains in same years • Opening year relief against total income of previous 3 tax years, FIFO basis • Carry forward relief against trading profits of same trade.	• Available against company profits only • Against total profits (income and gains) of current year • Carry back 12 months • Carry forward against trading profits of same trade

Withdrawal of funds	• No tax implications	• Salary/bonus versus dividend (see below)
		• Alternatives:
		   – Rent (but could affect eligibility to ER)
		   – Pension contributions

VAT	• Individual registers	• Company registers

	Sole trader (contd)	Company (contd)

Disposal of business interest	- Disposal of unincorporated business = gains on individual chargeable assets
	- Entrepreneurs' relief for CGT
	- If gifted:
	  - Gift relief available for CGT
	  - BPR available for IHT
	- If incorporated:
	  - Incorporation relief or
	  - Gift relief for CGT
		- Disposal of shares
		- Entrepreneurs' relief
		- If gifted:
		  - Gift relief for CGT may be available
		  - BPR for IHT may be available

Key Point

Where initial losses are anticipated, order events to ensure losses can be relieved against the individuals income and then incorporate business when it becomes profitable.

Extracting profits from a business

	Additional salary (i.e. bonus)	Dividend
Rates of income tax	IT liability = IT payable = 20%, 40% or 45%	IT liability = 10%, 32.5% or 37.5% of gross dividend with deemed tax credit of 10% Effective rate of IT payable on cash dividend received = 0%, 25%, 30.555%
NICs paid by individual	Class 1 primary at 12% or 2%	No NICs payable
NICs paid by company	Class 1 secondary at 13.8%	No NICs payable
Corporation tax implications	Salary and class 1 secondary NICs = allowable deductions for corporation tax	None
Pension contributions	Salary = relevant earnings for pension relief purposes	Dividends = not relevant earnings for pension relief purposes

Exam focus

Exam kit questions on this area:
- Bamburg Ltd

Disposal of interest in an unincorporated business

	Income tax	CGT	IHT
Sale of business	- Last adjustment of profits - Last capital allowances - BCs and BAs - Closing year rules applied	- Gains arise on every single chargeable asset - ROR - Entrepreneurs' relief	- No diminution in value - No IHT
Lifetime gift of business	As above	- Gains arise on every single chargeable asset - Gift relief - Entrepreneurs' relief	- PET or CLT - BPR = 100% Also available on death provided donee still owns business when donor dies
Death owning business	As above	- No CGT on death	- Business included in Death estate - BPR = 100%

Business finance and tax planning for companies

Incorporation of a business

Exam focus

Incorporation is a popular area for exam questions as it can test knowledge of all taxes in the syllabus:

- Income tax
- Corporation tax
- National insurance
- VAT
- SDLT
- Inheritance tax
- Capital gains tax

Exam focus

Exam kit questions on this area:

- Jerome and Tricycle Ltd
- Farina and Lauda

Chapter 18

Income tax
- Formerly profits of trade assessed to income tax
- Drawings and private use = not allowable deductions against profit
- Closing year rules apply on incorporation
- Balancing adjustments arise unless succession election applies
- If loss making Incorporation relief available (Chapter 13)

NICs
- Formerly liable to class 2 and class 4 NICs
- Now liable to class 1 primary
- Company liable to class 1 secondary and class 1 A NICs

Value Added Tax
Not a taxable supply
Provided conditions satisfied (Chapter 14)

Corporation tax
- Profits of trade now assessed to corporation tax
- Individual becomes director/shareholder
- Individual assessed to employment income and dividends
- Employment income and employers NICs = allowable deductions against profit

Incorporation

Capital gains tax
- Disposal of individual assets
- Incorporation relief or gift relief available (Chapter 6)

Inheritance tax
- No transfer of value
- No diminution in value

Stamp duty land tax
Payable by the company on purchase of land and buildings

Disincorporation

> **Definition**
>
> = the transfer of a company's trade and assets:
> - as a going concern
> - to one or more of its shareholders
> - who carry on the business as a sole trader or partnership, and
> - wind up the company.

Tax treatment

- the company's assets (tangible and intangible)
  = transferred to shareholders at open market value
  - large chargeable gains and income gains arise
  - assessed to CT

Disincorporation relief

From 1 April 2013 to 31 March 2018:

- a **joint claim** can be made (signed by company and shareholders) within **two years of the transfer**
- for qualifying business assets (**goodwill and interests in land and buildings**)
- to be transferred at:
  - goodwill = lower of TWDV or MV
  - interests in land = lower of cost or MV
- so no **immediate charge to CT** arises
- but shareholder acquires asset at the reduced base cost, and
- therefore the **gains = deferred** until the shareholder disposes of the asset transferred.

To qualify, **all** of the following conditions must be satisfied:

- the whole business = transferred as a going concern
- all of the business assets (with the exception of cash) = transferred to shareholders
- all of the shares = held by individuals
- the shareholders = held their shares for the 12 months preceding the transfer
- the total MV of qualifying assets ≤ £100,000.

Close companies

Close company = a company with close proprietorial control

(i.e. controlled by five or fewer shareholders or any number of directors usually a family company, an owner managed business)

1 Benefits provided to shareholders who are not employees

Shareholder	Close company
If shareholder = not an employee • Individual = treated as receiving a dividend • subject to income tax at 10%, 32.5% or 37.5% • 10% deemed tax credit applies • Value of the deemed cash dividend = the benefit which would have been assessable if they had been an employee of the company • Gross dividend = (assessable benefit × 100/90)	• Company = treated as paying a dividend to the shareholder • Costs of providing benefit = not allowable for the company • No class 1A NICs on deemed dividend
If shareholder = an employee • Individual = treated as receiving a normal benefit of employment	• Company = treated as giving a normal benefit to an employee • Costs of providing benefit = allowable for the company • Class 1A NICs payable

2 Loans provided to shareholders

Shareholder	Close company

• If loan is granted with a beneficial rate of interest, the loan benefit assessed as a beneficial loan (see benefits above)
• If the loan is written off by the company, the individual
= treated as receiving a cash dividend equivalent to the loan written off
• Subject to income tax at 10%, 32.5% or 37.5%
• 10% deemed tax credit applies
• Gross dividend
= (loan written off × 100/90)
	• Company must pay tax charge
	= 25% × loan advance if still outstanding at the normal due date (i.e. 9 months after end of the accounting period.)
	• Tax charge = payable on normal due date
	• Repaid 9 months after AP end in which
	  – loan repaid
	  – loan written off.
	• Tax charge does not apply if
	  1. Amount loaned ≤ £15,000
	  2. Individual = full time employee
	  3. Individual (with associates) owns < 5% interest in the company.

Business finance and tax planning for companies

3 Close investment company (CIC)
- Not qualifying interest i.e. not deductible.

4 Shareholder borrows money to buy shares in a close company
- Qualifying loan interest paid
  = allowable relief in shareholder's income tax computation
- reduces taxable income of individual.

Exam focus

Exam kit questions with close company aspects:
- Drench, Rain Ltd and Hail Ltd
- Banger Ltd and Candle Ltd
- Bamburg Ltd
- Nocturne Ltd

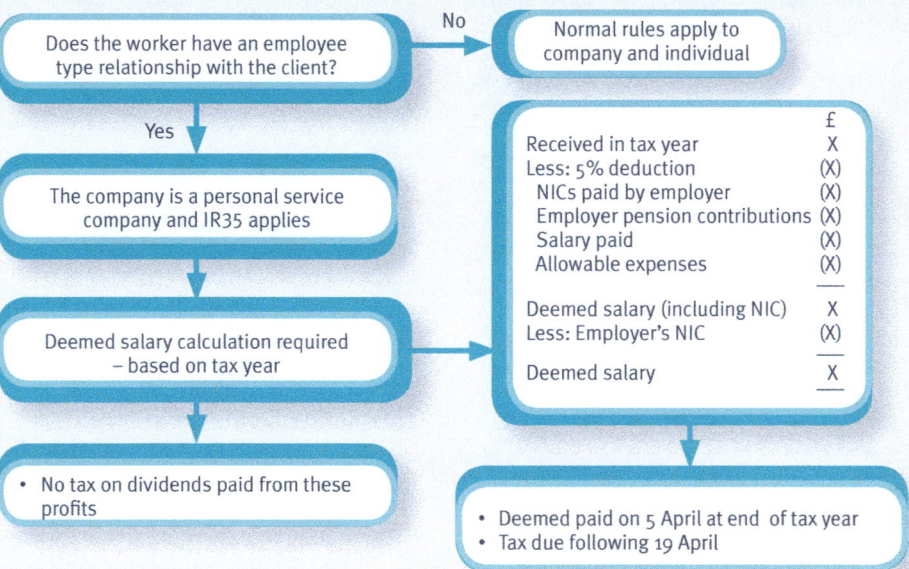

Exam focus

Exam kit questions on this area:

- Monisha and Horner

Chapter 18

Withdrawing investment

Withdrawing investment from a company

Sale of shares

- CGT – payable
- May be difficult to achieve as no ready market for unquoted shares

Purchase of own shares

- Conditions satisfied: – capital disposal liable to CGT and entrepreneurs' relief if personal trading company
- Conditions not satisfied: – treated as dividend = amount received less nominal value of shares

Liquidation of company

- Payments before liquidator appointed = income
- Payments after liquidator appointed = capital
- HMRC allows winding-up without a liquidator and payments to be treated as capital (max £25,000)

Purchase of own shares

Conditions for capital treatment:

(1) The company must be an unquoted trading company
(2) Be able to demonstrate that the repurchase of the shares is for the benefit of the trade and not part of a scheme to avoid tax.

    Examples of benefit to trade:
    - buying out retiring directors
    - buying out dissident shareholders
    - shareholder has died and beneficiaries don't want shares
    - venture capitalist withdrawing investment

(3) The individual must be resident in the UK
(4) Have owned the shares for 5 years prior to the repurchase
(5) Reduce their shareholding substantially after the buyback – the shareholder must end up with:
    - No more than 30% of the shares in the company, and
    - No more than 75% of the previous holding.

Exam focus

Exam kit questions with purchase of own shares:
- Spica
- Trifles Ltd, Victoria and Melba

Exam kit questions with liquidation:
- Banger Ltd and Candle Ltd

Chapter 18

Tax planning for companies

Investments to save tax
- Capital expenditure.
- R&D expenditure.

Tax planning
- Optimum use of losses.
- Group structure.
- Maximising group corporation tax reliefs.

Business finance and tax planning for companies

Index

Index

A

Above the line tax credit 269
Additional rate band 2
Additional tax on lifetime transfers as a result of donor's death 101
Adjusted total income 229
Agricultural property relief 106, 111
Amendments to the return 177
ANI 5
Annual accounting scheme 249
Annual allowance 40, 41
Annual exemption 106, 107
Annual Investment Allowance 207
Approved mileage allowance payments 20
Approved schemes 28
Arising basis 130
Assignment of a short lease 49
Assignment of leases 52
Augmented profits 279
Automatic non-UK residency tests 126
Automatic UK residency tests 126

B

Badges of trade 203
Balancing adjustments 209
Balancing payment 178
Baseline amount 114
Basic rate band 2
Beneficial loans 24
Benefits 18
Benefits on retirement 42
Bonus issues 60
Branch 312
Branch exemption election 314
Business property relief 106, 108
Business records 177
Business vehicle 329

C

Capital allowances 10, 12, 205, 223, 272
Capital allowances available for cars 210
Capital gains group 291, 299

Index

Capital gains tax planning 189
Capital goods scheme 254
Capital losses 53, 65, 288
Car benefit 21
Cash accounting scheme 247
Cash basis for small businesses 221
Cessation of business 223
CGT computation 46
Chargeable accounting periods 262
Chargeable Lifetime Transfers 97
Chattels 49, 51
Child benefit tax charge 8
Choice of accounting date 217
Class 1A 34, 35
Class 1 primary 34
Class 1 secondary 34, 35
Class 2 219
Class 4 219
Close companies 338
Close investment company 340
Closing year rules 223

Company residence 310
Compliance checks 184, 280
Conflicts of interest 162
Connected persons 54
Consortium 292
Consortium relief 298
Controlled foreign companies 316
CSOP 28

D

Dealing with HMRC 163
Death estate 102, 112
Debt versus Equity 326
Deed of variation 114, 117
Deemed domicile 145
Deemed occupation 74
Default interest 259
Default surcharge 257
Depreciating assets 78
Deregistration 241
Destination system 320

Diminution in value 103
Disaggregation 250
Discovery assessments 184
Discretionary trust 151
Dishonest conduct of tax agents 167
Disincorporation 336
Disincorporation relief 336
Dividends income 7
Domicile 125
Double tax relief 106, 115, 145

E

Effective rate of tax payable on dividends 13
EIS 6, 170, 172, 191
EIS reinvestment relief 68, 88
EMI 28, 71
Employee shareholder shares 30
Employment allowance 34, 35
Employment income 16
Employment versus self-employment 194
Entrepreneurs' relief 12, 68, 69, 77, 83

Error on VAT returns 258
Exempt assets 45
Exempt benefits 18
Exempt disposals 45
Exempt income 9
Exempt legacies 113
Ex-gratia compensation 33
Exit charge 155
Extracting profits from a business 332

F

Fall in value relief 107
Financing non-current assets 328
First year allowances 208
Flat rate expense deduction 222
Flat rate scheme 248
Foreign dividends 3
Franked investment income 279
Furnished holiday accommodation 12
Future test 239

Index

G

General anti-abuse rule 165
Gift of assets 25
Gift relief 12, 68, 80
Gifts with reservation 114
Giving advice to clients 168
Goodwill 266
Group payment arrangements 278
Group relief 291, 295, 304

H

Higher rate band 2
Hire purchase 328
Historic turnover test 239

I

IHT and CGT on sales/gifts 120
IHT computations 98
IIP trust 151, 154
Income tax computation 2
Income tax planning 189
Incorporation 334
Incorporation relief 68, 84
Individual savings accounts 9
Inheritance tax planning 190
Input tax 236
Input VAT 245
Intangibles 266
Intangibles rollover relief 266
Integral features 211
Investment products 170
IR35 341

J

Job-related accommodation 22, 23
Joint income 7
Joint tenants 105

K

Key investment products 170

Index

L

Large companies 278
Late payment interest 179, 278
Letting relief 68
Life assurance 105
Life tenant 151
Lifetime allowance 42
Lifetime gifts 97
Lifetime giving versus legacies on death 200
Lifetime tax 100
Liquidation 64, 343
Living accommodation 22
Loan relationship deficits 288
Loan relationships 265
Location of assets 146
Long period of account 275
Long term finance 326
Lump sum payments 33

M

Marriage Allowance 5
Married couples and civil partners 7, 55, 11
Married couples/civil partners tax planning 1
Matching rules 58
Maximum deduction from total income 4, 22
Mergers 62
Money laundering regulations 164

N

National insurance 34
National Insurance Contributions 219
New clients 161
Nil rate bands 99
Non-cash vouchers 18
Normal expenditure out of income 106
Notification of chargeability 176

Index

O

Occupational Pension Plans 39
Opening year rules 216
Opening years relief 227
Option to tax 251
Origin system 320
Other income 7
Output tax 236
Output VAT 243
Overseas aspects of VAT 320
Overseas branch 312
Overseas employment income 135
Overseas subsidiary 312

P

Parental dispositions 7
Part disposals 49, 50
Partial exemption 252
Partnerships 232
Patent box relief 267
Payment by instalments 56, 116
Payments on account 178
Payroll deduction scheme 17
Penalties 282
Pension income 42
Pensions 38
Personal allowance 4
Personal financial management 169
Personal Pension Plans 39
Personal service company 341
Potentially Exempt Transfers 97
Pre-entry loss 301
Premium for granting short leases 11
Pre-registration input VAT 246
Principal charge 155
Principal private residence relief 73
Private fuel 21
Private use assets 213
Professional Code of Ethics 160
Property income 10
Property income losses 288

Index

Publication of names of tax offenders 167
Purchase of own shares 343, 344

Q

QCB 63, 64
Qualifying charitable donations 264
Quarterly instalments 277
Quick succession relief 106, 115

R

Real estate investment trusts 13
Records 177
Reduction of PA 5
Redundancy payment 16
Related 51% group companies 291, 294
Related property 104
Relevant business property 108, 109
Relevant earnings 40
Relevant property trust 154
Remittance basis 131, 140
Remittance basis charge 133, 141

Rent-a-room relief 11
Repayment interest 9, 179, 278
Research and development expenditure 26
Residence 125
Restriction of carry forward of losses 287
Rights issues 60
Rollover relief 12, 68, 75, 300

S

Sale of rights (nil paid) 61
Sale of shares or assets 304
Savings income 3, 7
SAYE 9, 28
SEIS 6, 170, 172, 191
SEIS reinvestment relief 68, 89
Self-assessment 176, 234, 277
Senior accounting officers 281
Serious tax offenders 166
Settled property 113
Share for share exchange 62
Share options 26

Index

Share pool 59, 272
Share valuation rules 58
Short life assets 212
Short term finance 327
SIP 17, 29
Small gifts 106
Small part disposals 50
Small pool WDA 212
Sources of finance 175
Special rate pool 211
Splitting tax year 127, 128
Stamp duty 92, 93
Stamp duty land tax 92, 93
Stamp Duty Reserve Tax 92, 93
Standard penalties 180, 256
Substantial legacies to charity 114
Substantial shareholding exemption 270
Sufficient ties tests 126, 127

T

Takeovers 62, 63
Taper relief 102
Taxable total profits computation 263
Tax evasion versus tax avoidance 165
Tax Tribunals 186
Temporary absence abroad 143
Tenants in common 105
Terminal loss relief 228, 287
Termination payments 33
Trading losses 226, 283
Transfer of a going concern 244
Transfer of trade within a 75% group 306
Transfer of unused nil rate band 118
Transfer of value 103
Transfer pricing 307
Trust deed 150
Trustees 150
Trusts 150

Index

U

Use of assets 25

V

Valuation rules 58
Van benefit 21
VAT administration 256
VAT group registration 308
VAT penalties 256
VAT records 256
VAT registration 238
VAT returns 242
VCT 6, 9, 170, 172, 191
Vehicle benefits 21
Voluntary deregistration 241
Voluntary registration 240

W

Wasting chattels 51
Wear and tear allowance 10

Withdrawing investment 343
Writing down allowance 208